RAND | NATIONAL DEFENSE RESEARCH INSTITUTE

Assessing Retention and Special and Incentive Pays for Army and Navy Commissioned Officers in the Special Operations Forces

Beth J. Asch, Michael G. Mattock, James Hosek, Shanthi Nataraj

Prepared for the Office of the Secretary of Defense

Approved for public release; distribution unlimited

For more information on this publication, visit www.rand.org/t/RR1796

Library of Congress Cataloging-in-Publication Data is available for this publication.
ISBN: 978-0-8330-9880-1

Published by the RAND Corporation, Santa Monica, Calif.
© Copyright 2019 RAND Corporation
RAND® is a registered trademark.

Support RAND
Make a tax-deductible charitable contribution at
www.rand.org/giving/contribute

www.rand.org

Preface

Special and incentive (S&I) pays are used to create incentives for retention to meet military manning requirements. Although policymakers need a sound analytical and empirical basis for determining the effect of S&I pay changes on retention, no such capability currently exists for U.S. Special Operations Forces commissioned officers. This report, requested by the Office of Compensation within the Office of the Secretary of Defense, Personnel and Readiness, responds to this need. The report should interest policymakers responsible for setting and adjusting military compensation and maintaining Special Operations Forces capability. The report is a companion to a RAND report on the effect of S&I pays on the retention of officers in mental health care professions (Hosek, Nataraj, Mattock, and Asch, 2017). Both reports use a similar methodology—an adaptation of RAND's Dynamic Retention Model.

This research was conducted within the Forces and Resources Policy Center of the RAND National Defense Research Institute, a federally funded research and development center sponsored by the Office of the Secretary of Defense, the Joint Staff, the Unified Combatant Commands, the Navy, the Marine Corps, the defense agencies, and the defense Intelligence Community.

For more information on the Forces and Resources Policy Center, see www.rand.org/nsrd/ndri/centers/frp or contact the director (contact information is provided on the webpage).

Contents

Figures and Tables

Figures

Tables

Summary

U.S. Special Operations Forces (SOF) have been deployed intensively over the past 15 years, and this frequent use is expected to continue into the future. SOF members are highly selected and receive lengthy and costly training, making retention of those who qualify as SOF members a high priority. The focus of this report is on the retention of SOF commissioned officers and, specifically, on the effectiveness of monetary incentives, known as special and incentive (S&I) pays, for SOF officer retention. Historically, S&I pays have usually not been targeted to commissioned officers but to warrant officers and enlisted personnel. The objective of this research is to create a capability for predicting the effects of changes in the type or amount of S&I pay on SOF commissioned officer retention.

We used RAND's Dynamic Retention Model (DRM) as the analytical basis for relating S&I pay to retention. The DRM models an individual's retention and participation decisions over active and reserve careers. The DRM accounts for expected military and external earnings, allows for individual differences in the taste for military service and for random shocks in each period, and permits the individual to reoptimize depending on the conditions realized in a period. To extend the DRM to SOF personnel, we developed a database using Defense Manpower Data Center (DMDC) data that tracks the individual careers of SOF personnel. The data cover officer SOF entry cohorts into an active component from 1990 through 2000 and follow these cohorts through 2012. We used DMDC military and civilian pay data to compute expected military and civilian pay over an SOF career and gathered information on the types of S&I pay available to SOF officers to incorporate into the modeling. An important step was modifying the DRM to handle the SOF service member's choice of obligation length when offered multiyear special pay. We incorporated the obligation choices under the Special Warfare Officer Continuation Pay (SWOCP) and Critical Skills Retention Bonus (CSRB) programs, both of which have been used by the Navy. These programs were introduced to Navy officers during our data period, and not all entry cohorts had access to them at the same point in their careers, so we modified the DRM to vary the availability of the programs across calendar years and entry cohorts. As a result, retention profiles can differ for different SOF entry cohorts, which matches what we observed in our data.

We estimated models for SOF commissioned officers in the Navy and in the Army using the longitudinal retention database we created. We excluded the Marine Corps and Air Force because of insufficient data to enable modeling of SOF officers in these services. We found that nearly all the parameter estimates were statistically significant, and the model predictions fit the data well.

We used the estimated models, together with programs we developed for conducting policy simulations with the DRM, to simulate the retention effects of changes to S&I pay for SOF officers. The simulations show the steady-state retention effects in the active component resulting from alternative changes in S&I pay, specifically in the CSRB. The U.S. Department of Defense (DoD) authorized the CSRB program in 2005, but only the Navy has offered it to SOF officers. The CSRB is offered in two phases to qualified personnel. In Phase I, a qualified Navy SOF officer who has 15 to 18 years of service (YOS) can receive up to $25,000 per year for a five-year obligation, or less per year for a shorter obligation. In Phase II, a qualified Navy SOF officer who has 20 to 23 YOS can receive $15,000 per year for a five-year obligation and less per year for a shorter obligation. For the Navy, we simulated the retention effects of a 25-percent increase in the dollar amounts associated with each obligation contract length. For the Army, we simulated the effects of a policy offering Army SOF commissioned officers the CSRB program currently offered to Army SOF warrant officers.[1]

We found that offering the CSRB program to Army SOF officers would have a large effect on steady-state retention, increasing the size of the SOF officer force by 10.6 percent. The main increase in retention occurs among those with more than 19 YOS, substantially extending the careers of personnel who reach retirement eligibility at 20 YOS and might otherwise retire. The simulation shows the supply response of offering CSRB, assuming the Army permitted these individuals to stay. For the Navy, we found that increasing the dollar amounts under the existing CSRB program by 25 percent would increase the steady-state Navy SOF force by 3.7 percent. Most of the retention increase would occur among those with between 15 and 26 YOS, when members are eligible to receive the CSRB.

These simulations demonstrate the capability of the estimated DRM to simulate the steady-state retention effect of alternative changes in S&I pay. The capability we developed could be used to consider other changes, for instance, changing the dollar amounts and obligations under the existing SWOCP program in the Navy or offering a program like SWOCP to Army SOF personnel.

---

[1]   Army SOF warrant officers with 19 to 25 YOS can receive as much as $150,000 for a six-year obligation and as little as $18,000 for a two-year obligation.

Acknowledgments

We appreciate the support and guidance offered by Jerilyn Busch, Director, Office of Compensation (Office of the Secretary of Defense, Personnel and Readiness), and Bill Dougherty and Don Svendsen of that office. At RAND, Arthur Bullock assisted in database creation; Whitney Dudley provided research programming for civilian and military wage analysis; and Julia Pollak and Jonathan Wong wrote descriptions of SOF selection and career paths. John Warner's and Edward Keating's reviews of an earlier version of this report helped us improve it.

CHAPTER ONE

Introduction

The demand for U.S. Special Operations Forces (SOF) has been high and is expected to continue to be high in the future (Robinson, 2013). The demand is met by recruiting and retaining SOF members. This report focuses on the retention of SOF commissioned officers and, specifically, on the effectiveness of special and incentive (S&I) pays for increasing SOF officer retention.

Historically, S&I incentives have been directed to SOF enlisted personnel. In 2005, for example, the U.S. Department of Defense (DoD) approved a package of S&I pays for SOF personnel, including the Critical Skills Retention Bonus (CSRB), which targeted the retention of senior noncommissioned officers nearing retirement or who have met eligibility requirements for retirement. For the most part, S&I pays have not been targeted to commissioned officers. Army SOF officers are not eligible for the CSRB, while Navy SOF officers may receive the CSRB in specific subspecialties. Past research indicates that SOF enlisted personnel are responsive to S&I pays (Warner, 2012), but no evidence exists for officers.

The research in this report begins to fill this gap. We estimate dynamic retention models (DRM) for Army and Navy SOF officers, and these estimated models can be used to simulate the retention effects of changes in S&I pay. We demonstrate the simulation capability by showing the retention effects of offering a CRSB to Army SOF officers and of increasing CSRB amounts for Navy officers.

The DRM has been described extensively in past documents, including a recent document that develops and estimates DRMs for another critical officer skill area, mental health care providers (Hosek et al., 2017). The DRM uses longitudinal officer retention data to estimate parameters describing the distribution of officers' utility functions and the distribution of shocks that arise in each period. The estimated DRM can then be used to simulate alternative S&I pay policies, including policies not previously implemented. The DRM treats individual decisionmaking about whether to stay in the military or leave as a stochastic dynamic programming problem. An individual in the active component (AC) at a given point in his or her career evaluates the value of staying versus leaving. If the individual decides to leave, he or she works in the civilian economy and, each year, can decide whether to participate in a reserve component or not. The values of staying in the military or leaving depend on financial and nonfinancial factors. The financial factors reflect expected military and civilian compensation. Nonfinancial factors are represented by random shocks that occur on both the military and civilian sides and by individual preferences, or tastes, for military service, which differ across individuals. The values of staying or leaving also depend on the option value arising from being able to stay on active duty or leave in future periods if the decision in the current period is to stay. We estimate the parameters of the DRM with data on officer retention and reserve participation, giving the model an empirical grounding. Inputs into the estimation include information on expected military and civilian earnings over a career. We use the estimated DRM to demonstrate its capability to simulate the retention effect of changes in S&I pay.

This report is a companion to a RAND report on the effect of S&I pay on the retention of officers in the mental health care professions (Hosek et al., 2017). Both reports adapt the DRM and develop simulation capability to permit assessments of the retention effects of adjusting the level and structure of S&I pay targeted to their respective communities. In the companion report, the communities of interest are officers in mental health care occupations. In this report, we focus on officers in the special operations forces.

Organization of This Report

As background to our analysis, Chapter Two provides an overview of the SOF officer career in each service, and Appendix A provides more detail. Chapter Three describes the DRM and the method of estimation. Chapter Four describes the data and the military and civilian pay lines for SOF officers that are used as inputs in estimating the DRM. Chapter Five shows the DRM estimates and model fits, and Chapter Six presents simulations of the effect on retention of changes in S&I pay, specifically focusing on the CSRB. Chapter Seven offers our conclusions. Appendix B explains why we have not extended DRM to the Air Force and Marine Corps in this analysis.

Officer Special Operations Forces Careers and Special and Incentive Pays

In this chapter, we present an overview of AC career paths for commissioned officers whose occupational specialties are primarily considered to be U.S. Special Operations Command (USSOCOM) assets. These officers are expected to spend the majority of their careers in units that support USSOCOM.[1] These specialties are the ones included on our data analysis. Appendix A provides more detail on the requirements and career paths for SOF officers in each service and provides citations for the source material for this chapter. We incorporate key elements of these career paths into the DRM, as described in later chapters. We provide an overview for each service; however, our DRM analysis focuses only on the Army and Navy because available data are insufficient to model SOF careers in the Air Force and Marines, as discussed in Appendix B. The chapter also describes the S&I pays available to Army and Navy SOF officers. Table 2.1 summarizes key aspects of the Army and Navy SOF careers discussed in this chapter.

Table 2.1
Summary of Selected SOF Career Features in the Army and Navy

	Army	Navy
Occupations and branches[a]	Special operations (Green Berets) PSYOPS and CA	Naval Special Warfare Officers (SEALs)
YOS at entry	3 YOS	Entry
Training length	Qualification course: Varies, but typically 1 year to 18 months	BUDS/S training: 26 weeks Basic Airborne training: 3 weeks In-house training: 6 months
S&I pay	Dive Pay Jump Pay Demolition Pay Assignment Incentive Pay Foreign Language Proficiency Pay	Dive Pay Jump Pay Demolition Pay Assignment Incentive Pay Special Warfare Officer Continuation Pay CSRB Foreign Language Proficiency Pay

[a] See Chapter Four for the occupations for each service.

---

[1] As discussed in Appendix A, we do not include such units as Navy explosive ordinance disposal (EOD) teams and the Army's 75th Ranger Regiment because either these units do not directly support USSOCOM or their members do not spend the majority of their careers in SOF units. These individuals may qualify for certain S&I pays.

Career Overview by Service

Army

Army Special Forces (ARSOF) consists of three branches: Special Forces (SF), Psychological Operations (PSYOPS), and Civil Affairs (CA). Additionally, ARSOF units are also supported by soldiers from other branches and military occupational specialties (MOSs) that are not permanently part of ARSOF but rotate into ARSOF units (160th Special Operations Aviation Regiment and the 75th Ranger Regiment) on a temporary basis. We do not include these rotating MOS in our analyses.

SF officers, who are also known as Green Berets, plan, coordinate, direct, and participate in SF units performing foreign internal defense, direct action, special reconnaissance, counterterrorism, counterproliferation, and information operations missions. PSYOPS officers plan and execute information operations to influence the behavior of foreign target audiences. CA officers plan and execute missions that directly engage and influence foreign civilian populations through civil-military operations, such as populace and resource control, foreign humanitarian assistance, civil information management, support to civil administration, and nation assistance.

All three ARSOF branches recruit applicants from within the Army, generally selecting from officers with three years of service (YOS). Appendix A lists the minimum qualifications for each specialty. Applicants are reviewed by a centralized ARSOF screening board, and those selected are allowed time to complete their non-SOF requirements. Officers then go through a qualification course, typically in their fourth YOS, which varies in length and typically takes one year to 18 months. Once the officer has completed this course, he is considered a member of the SOF branch. Thus, SOF service typically begins in the fifth YOS.[2]

Active-duty service obligations (ADSOs) for joining ARSOF differ by specialty. SF officers incur a 36-month ADSO on graduation from the qualification course. This ADSO supersedes any prior service obligations. For instance, if an officer at the time of application had 72 months of remaining service obligation and passed the qualification course, his service commitment would be reduced to 36 months starting from his graduation date. PSYOPS and CA officers also incur a 36-month ADSO on graduation from the qualification course, but their ADSO runs concurrently with any prior service obligations. Thus, the officer would serve out the longest ADSO.

Navy

The Navy's primary contribution to USSOCOM is Naval Special Warfare (NSW) officers, better known as Sea-Air-Land (SEAL) officers. They are under the Naval Special Warfare Command. NSW officers plan, direct, and execute unconventional warfare (UW), direct action, counterterrorism, special reconnaissance, foreign internal defense, information warfare, security assistance, counterdrug operations, personnel recovery, and hydrographic reconnaissance missions.

NSW officers are accessed directly from their commissioning source (Officer Candidate School, Naval Reserve Officers Training Corps [ROTC], U.S. Naval Academy) or, in limited

---

[2]   As we discuss in the next chapter, we limit our sample of officers to those who are first observed as Army SOF between YOS 4.5 and 6.5. Consequently, we do not model the decision to stay in service before YOS 4.5 and join ARSOF. That is, our analysis of retention is conditional on joining SOF.

numbers, via lateral transfers within the Navy. Lateral transfers must be an O-1 or O-2 at the time of application and must be qualified in a warfare specialty. In rare cases, NSW officers are accessed via interservice academy transfers (U.S. Military Academy, U.S. Air Force Academy, etc.) and interservice lateral transfers. Appendix A lists specific qualifications for applicants.

Applicants selected for training undergo Basic Underwater Demolition/SEAL (BUD/S) training (26 weeks) and Basic Airborne Training (three weeks). On graduation, they are assigned to a SEAL Delivery Vehicle Team or SEAL Team. After a six-month in-house training and observation period, NSW officers are evaluated, and their performance is reviewed by their commanding officers. The designators of those found qualified are changed from 118X (SEAL Trainee) to 113X (SEAL). Those found unqualified are placed in a probationary status for at least six months and then be reevaluated, or they become available for reassignment and their NSW designation and/or additional qualifying designation is revoked. An officer who applies to become a SEAL incurs an ADSO of three years on completion of BUD/S and Basic Airborne Training.

Air Force

The Air Force contributes several types of commissioned officers to the special operations community: Special Operations Pilots, Special Operations Combat System Officers, Special Tactics Officers (STOs), Combat Rescue Officers, Special Operations Remotely Piloted Aircraft (RPA) Pilots, and Special Operations Weather Officers.[3]

Special operations pilots fly fixed- and rotary-wing aircraft to support special operations mission sets such as UW, counterterrorism, direct action, and special reconnaissance. Special Operations Combat System Officers are flying officers trained to perform the duties of a combat systems officer, fire control officer, or electronic warfare officer in support of special operations mission sets. STOs plan and execute ground missions, such as assault zone assessment and control, fire support, personnel recovery, combat search and rescue, battlefield trauma care, and tactical weather operations. Combat Rescue Officers are nonrated aircrew officers who lead and command personnel recovery operations as direct combatants. They perform duties as mission planners and provide personnel recovery expertise to command and battle staffs on recovery operations, including survival, evasion, resistance, and escape programs. Special Operations RPA Pilots are officers trained to operate specialized mission aircraft and command flight crews to accomplish special operations, combat, training, and other missions.[4] Special Operations Weather Officers command, manage, and perform weather operations for Air Force and Army support organizations activities.

All prospective Air Force special operations officers may be directly accessed via Officer Training School (OTS), Air Force ROTC, or U.S. Air Force Academy or can be transferred from other communities. Across the accession sources, candidates can volunteer for rated positions through a similar process.[5] For each career field, the top candidates are selected until all

---

[3]   In addition, other officers, such as intelligence officers and pilots serving as Combat Aviation Advisors, may be selected to serve temporarily in the Air Force Special Operations Command (AFSOC), but are not discussed here.

[4]   Regular RPA Pilots with the Air Force Specialty Code (AFSC) 11UX can receive specialized training in special operations and attain the suffix S, signifying that they are qualified in special operations.

[5]   In Air Force ROTC, for example, candidates typically choose the rated position for which they want to volunteer during their junior year in college. They do so by providing a ranked list of the rated fields for which they would like to be consid-

positions are filled. The remaining candidates are then considered for the next position for which they volunteered.

Unlike Army and Navy SOF accessions, the point in a career at which an officer enters the SOF community can vary widely. In addition, the length of training differs widely across specialties, ranging from 53 days for weather officers to 882 days for special operations pilots. As we discuss in Appendix B, this variability poses challenges when we estimate a DRM for the Air Force and would require a significant expansion of the DRM capability. Consequently, we do not estimate a DRM for the Air Force SOF officer community. Appendix A provides further details on accession requirements and training by specialty. Officers typically incur a six-year ADSC on graduation.

Marines

The Marine Corps began contributing forces to USSOCOM in the mid-2000s and is in the process of building the Marine Corps Special Operations Command (MARSOC). At the time of this writing, MARSOC was defining the career path for its Special Operations Officers. Given the time frame of our analysis and the evolving nature of the Marine Corps SOF community, we have not included Marine Corps officers in our analysis. Appendix A provides details on the qualification requirements and accessions for the Critical Skills Operator specialty. Appendix B discusses our exclusion of the Marine Corps in our analysis.

Special and Incentive Pays for Army and Navy Special Operations Forces Officers

This subsection discusses the S&I pays that could be paid to SOF personnel, though, in some cases, the services may opt not to pay them to officers. The rules governing this are set out in *DoD Financial Management Regulation*, Vol. 7A: *Military Pay Policy–Active Duty and Reserve Pay* (DoD 7000.14-R). Both Navy and Army SOF officers can receive a variety of S&I pays that reflect assignments, special duties, hazardous duties, and proficiencies associated with SOF specialties. Qualified SOF officers can receive Dive Pay equal to $240 per month. SOF officers are also entitled to Jump or Parachute Pay if they are qualified. Those qualified in static line jump (parachuting) operations receive $150 per month, while those qualified in high altitude low opening (free fall) operations receive $225 per month. Those who complete monthly demolition qualifications receive $150 per month of Demolition Pay. SOF officers may also receive Assignment Incentive Pay; special mission unit (SMU) operators with fewer than 25 YOS are eligible for $750 per month if they have fewer than three YOS as an SMU operator, or $1,000 per month if they have three or more YOS as an SMU operator.

In addition, some SOF officers may be offered continuation or retention incentive pays associated with multiyear service commitments. Since 1999, all officers in the SOF community can receive Special Warfare Officer Continuation Pay (SWOCP), although only the Navy currently offers SWOCP to its officers. SWOCP is offered to those with six through 14 YOS, and the bonus is $15,000 per year for a five-year obligation; $12,500 per year for four years;

---

ered. Selection decisions are made in the following order: (1) traditional pilot positions, (2) RPA pilot positions, (3) combat systems operators (formerly called *navigators*), and (4) air battle managers.

$10,000 per year for three years; and $6,000 for one year (Chief of Naval Operations Instruction 7220.16A, 2015). Thus, a longer commitment pays a higher amount per year.

DoD authorized the payment of the CSRB to members of the SOF community in 2005, yet until 2007, only enlisted members and warrant officers were eligible for the CSRB. The authorization sets the maximum, and the services can set bonus amounts up to this maximum. The Navy began offering the CSRB to special warfare officers in 2007 and updated the offer in 2013 (Bureau of Naval Personnel, 2014). The Army does not offer the CSRB to SOF commissioned officers, only to SOF enlisted personnel and warrant officers.

The Navy CSRB program for special warfare personnel is offered in two phases. In Phase 1, an SOF officer in the 1130 designator, who has been screened for a commanding officer or executive officer tour, and who has between 15 and 18 YOS can receive up $25,000 per year for a five-year obligation or $15,000 per year for a three-year obligation. Also in Phase 1, an SOF officer in the 1137 designator can receive $20,000 per year for a five-year obligation or $10,000 per year for a three-year obligation. In Phase 2, an SOF officer in designator 1130 who has screened for a commanding officer tour and has between 20 and 23 YOS can receive $15,000 per year for a five-year commitment or $10,000 for a three-year commitment. These pays have a significant impact on retention, as shown in Chapter Six.

CHAPTER THREE

Overview of the Dynamic Retention Model and the Estimation Methodology

The DRM is a model of the decision, made each year, to stay in the AC or leave and, for those who leave, to participate in a reserve component or not. Retention decisionmaking is structured as a dynamic program in which the individual seeks to choose the best career path, but the path is subject to uncertainty. The model is formulated in terms of parameters that are estimated with retention data and then used to see how well the estimated model fits observed retention. We also use the estimated parameters in policy simulations. In the case of SOF personnel, we considered counterfactual S&I pay policies.

This chapter presents an overview of the DRM for Navy and Army SOF officers. Our description follows that in a companion report on mental health care providers (Hosek et al., 2017) and draws from our DRM analysis of Air Force pilot retention (Mattock et al., 2016).

Since Army SOF officers can typically apply to be in SOF with three YOS, and training takes place during the fourth YOS, the DRM for Army SOF officers begins when the officer begins making retention decisions as a SOF officer at YOS 5 or 6. Since Navy officers begin in SOF at entry, the model for Navy SOF officers begins at entry. In each year, the SOF officer can choose to continue in the AC or to leave the AC. An individual leaving active duty can decide whether to hold only a civilian job or to hold a civilian job and also to participate in a reserve component. Once having left active duty, the individual cannot return to it but can move back and forth between the reserve and civilian states.

We denote the value of staying in the AC at time t as

$$V_t^S = V_t^A + \varepsilon_t^A,$$

where V_t^A is the nonstochastic value of the active alternative, and ε_t^A is a random shock. The value of leaving at time t is

$$V_t^L = \max\left[V_t^R + \omega_t^R, V_t^C + \omega_t^C\right] + \varepsilon_t^L,$$

where the member can choose between reserve and civilian. *Civilian* means working at a non-military job, and *reserve* means participating in a reserve component and working at a non-military job. The value of reserve is given by $V_t^R + \omega_t^R$, while the value of civilian is given by $V_t^C + \omega_t^C$. We model the reserve-civilian choice as a nest and assume that the stochastic terms follow an extreme value type I distribution, which leads to a nested logit specification.[1] The

---

[1] See Train, 2009, for a discussion of the logit and nested logit specifications.

within-nest shocks to the reserve/civilian choice are given by ω_t^R and ω_t^C, while the nest-level shock is given by ε_t^L.

The shock terms represent a variety of possible events, such as a good assignment, dangerous mission, strong civilian job market, opportunity for promotion, new location, change in marital status, change in dependency status, change in health status, or the prospect of deployment or deployment itself. We allow a common shock for the reserve and civilian nest, ε_t^L, since an individual in the reserves also holds a civilian job, as well as shock terms specific to the reserve and civilian states, ω_t^R and ω_t^C. The individual is assumed to know the distributions that generate the shocks and the shock realizations in the current period but not in future periods. The distributions are assumed to be constant over time, and the shocks are uncorrelated within and between periods. Once a future year is reached, and the shocks are realized, the individual can reoptimize, i.e., choose the alternative with the maximum value at that time. But in the current period, the future realizations are not known, so the individual assesses the future period by taking the expected value of the maximum, i.e., the expected value of civilian conditional on it being superior to that of reserve times the probability of that occurring, plus the expected value of reserve conditional on it being superior to civilian times the probability of that occurring. For instance, depending on the shocks and the compensation, there is some chance that V_t^S will be greater than V_t^L, in which case V_t^S would be the maximum, and vice versa, and the individual makes an assessment of the expected value of the maximum, $E\max\left(V_t^S, V_t^L\right)$.

The extreme value distribution, denoted EV, has location parameter a and scale parameter b; the mean is $a + b\phi$, and the variance is $\pi^2 b^2/6$, where ϕ is Euler's gamma (~0.577). As we derived in past studies, this implies

$$\varepsilon_t^{Leave} \sim EV\left[-\phi\sqrt{\lambda^2+\tau^2}, \sqrt{\lambda^2+\tau^2}\right]$$
$$\omega_t^R \sim EV\left[-\phi\lambda, \lambda\right]$$
$$\omega_t^C \sim EV\left[-\phi\lambda, \lambda\right]$$
$$\varepsilon_t^L \sim EV\left[-\phi\tau, \tau\right],$$

where λ is the common scale parameter of the distributions of ω_t^R and ω_t^C, and τ is the scale parameter of the distribution of ε_t^L. In the nested structure of the model, leavers face a common shock for the "leave" nest, ε_t^L, as well as shocks for the reserve and civilian alternatives within the nest, ω_t^R and ω_t^C, which all together produce a leave shock distributed as extreme value type I, with location parameter,

$$-\phi\sqrt{\lambda^2+\tau^2},$$

and scale parameter,

$$\sqrt{\lambda^2+\tau^2}.$$

The logit model requires that the scale parameters of the leave and stay shocks be equal, so we parameterize the model such that the stay scale parameter, which we denote κ, has the same value as the leave scale parameter, i.e.,

$$\kappa = \sqrt{\lambda^2+\tau^2}.$$

The values of the alternatives V_t^A, V_t^R and V_t^C depend on the current pay for serving in an AC or working as a civilian, W_t^a or W_t^c. If the individual is a reservist, he earns the civilian wage plus reserve pay, $W_t^c + W_t^r$. In addition, each individual has tastes for active and reserve duty, γ_a and γ_r respectively, which also enter the value functions for active and reserve service. Each taste represents the individual's perceived net advantage of holding an active or reserve position, relative to the civilian state. Other things equal, a higher taste for active or reserve service increases retention. The tastes are assumed to be constant over time but vary across individuals. Also, tastes for active and reserve service are not observed but are assumed to follow a bivariate normal distribution over AC entrants.

The nonstochastic part of the value of staying active, V_t^A, can therefore be written as

$$V_t^A = \gamma_a + W_t^a + \beta E\left[\max\left(V_{t+1}^L, V_{t+1}^S\right)\right],$$

where β is the personal discount factor.

The possibility of reoptimizing in future periods distinguishes dynamic programming models from other dynamic models. Reoptimization means that the individual can choose the best alternative in a period when its conditions have been realized, i.e., when the shocks are known. As mentioned, future realizations are unknown in the current period, and the best the individual can do is to estimate the expected value of the best choice in the next period, i.e., the expected value of the maximum. This will also be true in the following period, and the one after it, and so forth, so the model is forward-looking and rationally handles future uncertainty. Thus, today's decision takes into account the possibility of future changes of state and assumes that future decisions will also be optimizing.

The nonstochastic values of the reserve choice and civilian choice can be written as

$$V_t^R = \gamma_r + W_t^c + W_t^r + \beta E\left[\max\left[V_{t+1}^R + \omega_t^R, V_{t+1}^C + \omega_t^C\right]\right]$$

$$V_t^C = W_t^c + R_t + \beta E\left[\max\left[V_{t+1}^R + \omega_t^R, V_{t+1}^C + \omega_t^C\right]\right]$$

where R_t in the civilian equation is the present value of any active or reserve military retirement benefit for which the individual is eligible.

The model has two switching costs. *Switching cost* refers to a de facto cost reflecting the presence of constraints or barriers affecting the movement from particular states and periods to other states, relative to the movement that would otherwise have been expected from the expressions shown above for V_t^A, V_t^R, and V_t^C plus their respective shock terms. Switching costs are not actually paid by the individual but, as estimated in the model, are a monetary representation of the constraints or barriers affecting the transition from one state to another at a given time. Further, a switching cost can be either negative or positive. A negative value implies a loss to the individual when changing from the current status to an alternative status, while a positive value implies a gain, or incentive, for the change. The first switching cost is a cost of leaving the AC before the ADSO is completed. For the Army, for example, an officer entering SOF at YOS 5 has an ADSO of four years at that point, and the first switching cost covers YOS 5 through 8. For the Navy, SOF training is in the first year and the first switching cost covers the four-year ADSO from YOS 2 through 5. The estimates in Chapter Five indicate that the switching cost has a negative value for the Army and the Navy. This might reflect the perceived cost of breaching the ADSO contract. The second switching cost is a cost of switching into the reserve from the civilian state. This cost could represent difficulty in finding a reserve position in a desired geographic location or an adverse impact on one's civilian job, e.g., from not being available to work on certain weekends or for two weeks in the summer or being subject to reserve call-up. Its estimated value is negative for the Army and the Navy.

The individual does not know when future military promotions will occur, but we assume that the individual knows the promotion policy and pay scales and forms an expectation of military pay in future periods. Similarly, the individual forms an expectation of civilian pay. We discuss the development of the expected military and civilian pay profiles in Chapter Four.

Extending the Model to Handle Special and Incentive Pays Entailing a Service Obligation

As described in Chapter Two, SOF officers receive a variety of special incentives to reflect the assignments, special or hazardous duties, and proficiencies of their service, such as Dive Pay and Parachute Pay. These are currently the only pays that Army SOF officers may receive, but selected Navy SOF officers are eligible for retention-related incentives, specifically SWOCP and CSRB. The amount of these incentives depends on the length of the service obligation the member chooses. The Navy did not offer SWOCP before 1999 and did not offer CSRB to Navy officers until 2007, and the CSRB offer changed in 2013. Consequently, these multiyear contracts initially became available at different YOS for officers from different entry cohorts.

We can handle S&I pays, such as Dive Pay, that do not depend on a choice of service obligation by incorporating the S&I amount into average military pay for the Army, as we describe in the next chapter. In the case of the Navy, we used regular military compensation (RMC) for the pay line. SWOCP and CSRB, however, call for an extension of the DRM to allow members to make choices over a menu of obligation lengths with associated pay amounts. Further, modeling when during his career a given officer faces the SWOCP and CSRB choices also calls for an extension of the DRM to allow these choices to vary by entry cohort. We infer calendar year in the model and, hence, the bonus values under SWOCP and CSRB that vary with calendar year from the entry cohort date and other time clocks in the model, such as active YOS.

We extended the DRM in a fashion similar to the modeling in Mattock et al. (2016), in which we incorporated the Air Force pilot's choice of a multiyear contract under the Aviation Continuation Pay (ACP) program.[2] In that model, rated personnel who choose a longer contract receive ACP for more years, and their multiyear contract means that they forgo the opportunity to take advantage of attractive opportunities that might present themselves during the contract period. This multiyear contract length choice is modeled as a nested choice made under uncertainty. The uncertainty arises in the Air Force model from not knowing the specific future conditions (e.g., assignments, flying time, deployments) that accompany these choices. The incorporation of this nested ACP contract length choice required estimation of an additional parameter in the model, related to the variance of the shock associated with the

---

[2]   We take a similar approach in our companion paper (Hosek et al., 2017), where we incorporate the choice of multiyear special pay obligation into the DRM for psychiatrists. However, the model for psychiatrists did not recognize different entry cohorts and also did not allow the multiyear special pay choice set to vary with calendar year.

multiyear contract choice. As with the Navy SOF community, the ACP choice set has varied over time in the Air Force. Consequently, in the DRM for Air Force pilots, we allowed the model to consider entry cohorts separately, thereby allowing us to incorporate ACP policy changes that occurred over the data period.

We followed a similar approach in extending the DRM to incorporate SWOCP and CSRB for SOF personnel. That is, we modeled the SWOCP and CSRB contract length choices as nested choices made under uncertainty and allowed the choice set to vary across calendar year by considering entry cohorts separately. We incorporated the SWOCP and CSRB choices into both the estimation computer code and the simulation code for the Navy. For the Army, we incorporated the S&I pay/obligation choice into the simulation code but not the estimation code. (As mentioned, the Army has not made use of SWOCP or CSRB for officers.) Since the estimation code for the Army does not include this choice, we did not estimate an additional parameter related to the variance of the shock associated with the multiyear contract choice, as we did for the Navy. Consequently, for the Army, we assumed that the variance is zero.

We included the SWOCP and CSRB choices by adding equations that express the value of the SWOCP and CSRB programs for different obligation lengths. The DRM described above involves two equations. The first is the value of staying active, and the second is the value of leaving, which is a nest of the reserve and civilian choice. Because our focus is on the multiyear choice while a member is in the AC, we ignore the nest and describe the value of leaving simply as V_t^L.

The equation V_t^S gives the value of staying active for one additional year, at time t. Thus, we can write the value of staying active for one more year as

$$V_t^{S/1} = V_t^{A/1} + \varepsilon_t^A = \gamma_a + W_t^a + \beta E\left[\max\left(V_{t+1}^L, V_{t+1}^S\right)\right] + \varepsilon_t^{A/1},$$

where W_t^a for those with between six and 14 YOS at time t now includes the SWOCP available to eligible Navy personnel who stay for one year. Note that CSRB for eligible Navy SOF officers does not include a payment for staying one year. Also, because the SWOCP and CSRB contract offer varies with calendar year, we introduced entry cohort date as an additional time clock, so that W_t^a and therefore V_t^S depend on entry cohort c as well as t. We can therefore write W_t^a as $W_{t,c}^a$ and V_t^S as $V_{t,c}^S$. However, to reduce the clutter of notation, we omit the cohort subscripts in what follows.

We can write the value of staying active and taking the SWOCP with a three-year obligation as

$$V_t^{S/3} = V_t^{A/3} + \varepsilon_t^A = \sum_{n=0}^{2} \beta^n \left[\gamma_a + W_{t+n}^a\right] + \beta^3 E\left[\max\left(V_{t+3}^L, V_{t+3}^S\right)\right] + \varepsilon_t^{A/3}.$$

This equation also applies to those eligible for CSRB (Phases I and II) who take a three-year obligation, with the difference that t differs because CSRB is targeted to those later in the SOF career. The shocks in the intervening periods covered by the commitment are inconsequential because there is no stay-or-leave choice to be made, and the expected value of the shock in each period is zero. In contrast, in a future period when a choice can be made, the better alternative will be chosen, and it is evaluated in the current period as the expected value of the maximum of that future choice.

Similarly, the value staying active and taking SWOCP or CSRB with a *k*-year obligation is

$$V_t^{S/k} = V_t^{A/k} + \varepsilon_t^A = \sum_{n=0}^{k-1} \beta^n \left[\gamma_a + W_{t+n}^a \right] + \beta^k E\left[\max\left(V_{t+k}^L, V_{t+k}^S \right) \right] + \varepsilon_t^{A/k}.$$

An eligible Navy SOF officer compares the value of leaving, V_t^L, with the maximum of the value of staying for one year, $V_t^{S/1}$, three years, $V_t^{S/3}$, or *k* years, where *k* can equal one, three, four, or five in the case of SWOCP. In the case of CSRB, an incentive is only offered for an obligation of three or five years, so *k* can equal three or five.

For the Navy SWOCP, the probability that an initially offered SOF officer will stay active is

$$\Pr\left[\max\left(V_t^{S/1}, V_t^{S/3}, V_t^{S/4}, V_t^{S/5} \right) > V^L \right].$$

For the Navy CSRB, the probability that an initially offered SOF officer will stay active is

$$\Pr\left[\max\left(V_t^{S/1}, V_t^{S/3}, V_t^{S/5} \right) > V^L \right].$$

Recall that there is no incentive under the Navy CSRB for taking a one-year contract.

As with the reserve/civilian choice, the SWOCP and CSRB obligation choices could be handled as a nested choice. If we assume the random shocks of these choices follow an extreme value distribution, we can write

$$\varepsilon_t^{A/k} \sim EV\left(-\phi\lambda_2, \lambda_2 \right),$$

where λ_2 is the scale parameter and is subscripted with 2 to distinguish it from the shape parameter for the within–reserve/civilian nest shock, defined above, which we now denote as λ_1, e.g.,

$$\omega_t^R \sim EV\left[-\phi\lambda_1, \lambda_1 \right]$$

Thus, the SWOCP and CSRB choices add an additional parameter to be estimated for the Navy model. For the Army model, we do not include this additional parameter (λ_2 is set to zero).

Also, like the reserve/civilian choice, members may have the option to make multiple contract choices over their careers. For example, they might choose a one-year contract at first, then choose a five-year contract, and then follow that with a three-year contract before leaving. Because our data do not indicate which contract choice Navy SOF officers made or the sequence of contract choices, we instead calculated the probability of observing an SOF officer staying a particular number of years and then leaving or being censored (i.e., the data end before the officer leaves) by summing up all possible sequences of contract decisions for the purposes of constructing the likelihood function. As discussed in Mattock et al. (2016), most paths have a near-zero probability. We exploited this fact in our calculations by noting that, if one term of a product of probabilities is zero, the entire expression is zero. This saves us from explicitly having to calculate the other terms in the cumulative probability expression.

Extending the Model to Recognize Variability in Retention Over Time

SOF officer retention has varied over time for both the Navy and the Army as seen in Figures 3.1 and 3.2, respectively. The figures show the cumulative retention rate through 2012 for each cohort entering SOF from 1990 to 2000. The data used are described in more detail in Chapter Four. For most Navy cohorts, the percentage of the entry cohort reaching YOS 10 varies from about 40 percent for the 1997 cohort to about 85 percent for the 1999 cohort. The 2000 cohort and 1995 cohorts are outliers. For most Army cohorts, the cumulative retention profile is relatively similar among cohorts that entered SOF in the early 1990s (e.g., 1990 to 1996 cohorts), but retention is higher in more recent cohorts, especially the 1999 and 2000 cohorts.

In addition, Army and Navy SOF strengths have varied over time. Figure 3.3 shows the SOF strength from 2002 to 2012, based on the pay data described in the next chapter. Strength increased in both services, although Navy strength was relatively stable between 2006 and 2011. Still, in both services, both the experience mix, as indicated by the retention profiles, and the size of the force have changed over time. The SOF forces have become more experienced and larger.

The variability over time in the retention profiles and sizes of the SOF forces poses a problem in estimating the DRM. If we pooled the data across cohorts, the estimated parameters could be influenced by cross-cohort retention differences and not reflect retention behavior for a given individual over a career. Addressing this issue required extending the DRM to

Figure 3.1
Navy SOF Officer Active Component Cumulative Retention Rate, by Year Cohort Entered SOF

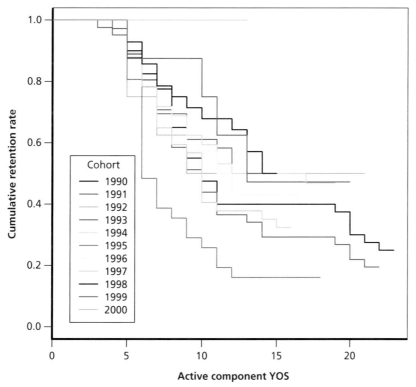

SOURCE: Authors' computations using the Defense Manpower Data Center's (DMDC's) Work Experience File (WEX) (see Chapter Four for description).
RAND *RR1796-3.1*

Figure 3.2
Army SOF Officer Active Component Cumulative Retention Rate, by Year Cohort Entered SOF

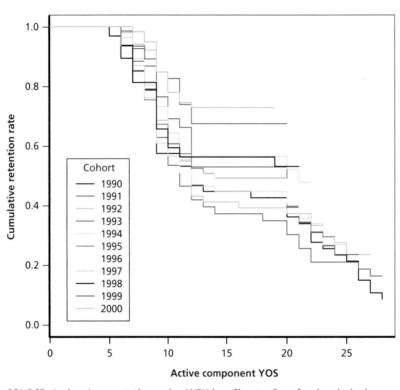

SOURCE: Authors' computations using WEX (see Chapter Four for description).
RAND *RR1796-3.2*

account for variability across cohorts. A similar issue arose in our DRM modeling for U.S. Coast Guard enlisted personnel (Asch, Mattock, Hosek, 2017), and we have applied the methodology here that we developed to address this issue for the Coast Guard.

To the extent possible, we would like to take advantage of all the historical data available when estimating a retention model because earlier cohorts give us insight into how people make decisions throughout their careers, while more recent cohorts can only give us insight into the early part of a career. Mid- through late-career data are particularly valuable because these tend to be the years when the possibility of collecting the defined-benefit retirement annuity at 20 YOS weighs most heavily on people's minds. While the retention experience of more-recent cohorts may be closer to what we expect to see in the near future for SOF officers, recent cohort data alone do not cover enough YOS to allow us to confidently estimate the retention model parameters.

The approach we have taken is to allow the value of staying, V^A, to vary over time as a function of SOF end strength, $S(year)$, where *year* refers to calendar year. The underlying idea is that the attractiveness of staying in SOF will vary positively with end strength because this will mean that there are more opportunities in higher YOS for these personnel. Strength enters into the value of staying as an additive term multiplied by the coefficient δ. Given an individual's entry cohort and YOS, we can calculate the calendar year and so obtain the end strength for that year, as $S(year) = S(cohort + t_{active} - 1)$. The value of staying for SOF then becomes

$$V_t^A = \gamma_a + \delta S(\text{cohort} + t - 1) + W_t^a + \beta E\left[max\left[V_{t+1}^L, V_{t+1}^S \right]\right]$$

Figure 3.3
Army and Navy AC SOF Strength by Year

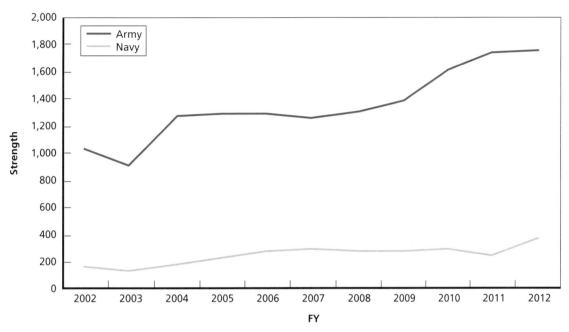

SOURCE: Authors' computations using DMDC Pay Files (see Chapter Four for description).
RAND RR1796-3.3

The value of staying now depends on entry cohort, as is the case described earlier, where we extended the DRM to handle S&I pay that varies over time.

This approach works well for the Army, as can be seen in the fit chart in Chapter Five. Furthermore, the estimated coefficient on end strength is positive and significant for the Army, as expected. For the Navy, the coefficient is not significant, and the model fit is poorer than when we use a model that assumes δ is zero. Consequently, for the Navy, we report results assuming δ is zero. In retrospect, this finding is perhaps not surprising. Army SOF strength rose fairly steadily from 2002 through 2012, while Navy SOF strength changed little from 2006 to 2011 (Figure 3.3).

Estimation Methodology

To estimate DRMs for Army and Navy SOF officers, we used the mathematical structure of the DRM, together with assumptions on the distributions of tastes and shocks. This allowed us to derive expressions for the transition probabilities, given one's state, which we then used to obtain an expression for the likelihood of each individual's years of active retention and reserve participation. Importantly, each transition probability is itself a function of the underlying parameters of the DRM. These are the parameters of the taste distribution, the shock distributions, the switching costs, and the discount factor. The estimation routine finds the set of parameter values that maximize the overall sample likelihood for all the individual SOF careers we observe.

The transition probability is the probability in a given period of choosing a particular alternative, i.e., active, reserve, or civilian, given one's state. Because we assumed the model is first-order Markov[3] and that the shocks have extreme value distributions and are uncorrelated from year to year, we can derive closed-form expressions for each transition probability. For example, the probability of choosing to stay active at time t, given that the member is already in the AC, is given by the logistic form

$$\Pr\left(V^A > V^L\right) = \frac{e^{\frac{V^A}{\kappa}}}{e^{\frac{V^A}{\kappa}} + \left(e^{\frac{V^R}{\lambda}} + e^{\frac{V^C}{\lambda}}\right)^{\frac{\lambda}{\kappa}}}.$$

(We omit the subscripts for individual i and year t.) We can also obtain expressions for the probability of leaving the AC and, having left, the probabilities of entering, or staying in, the reserve component in each subsequent year. To relate the DRM to discrete choice models, we note that, in a given period and for a given state and individual taste, the individual's value functions for staying and leaving have the same form as those of a random utility model. Similarly, for those who have left the AC, the choices of whether to enter the reserves or to remain in the reserves are also based on a random utility model. More broadly, the reserve choice is nested in the choice to leave the AC, and the model has a nested logit form. (See Train, 2009, for further discussion.) Of course, the DRM differs from a traditional random utility model because the explanatory variables are value functions, not simple variables, such as age and education, and the value functions are recursive.

The transition probabilities in different periods are independent and can be multiplied together to obtain the probability of any given individual's career profile of active, reserve, and civilian states that we observed in the data. Multiplying the career profile probabilities together gives an expression for the sample likelihood that we used to estimate the model parameters for each occupation using maximum likelihood methods. Optimization was done using the Broyden-Fletcher-Goldfarb-Shanno algorithm, a standard hill-climbing method. We computed standard errors of the estimates using numerical differentiation of the likelihood function and taking the square root of the absolute value of the diagonal of the inverse of the Hessian matrix. To judge goodness of fit, we used parameter estimates to simulate retention profiles for synthetic individuals (characterized by tastes drawn from the taste distribution) who are subject to shocks (drawn from the shock distributions), then aggregated the individual profiles to obtain a force-level retention curve and compared it with the retention curve computed from actual data.

We estimated the following model parameters:

- mean and standard deviation of tastes for active and reserve service relative to civilian opportunities (e.g., μ_a, μ_r, σ_a, σ_r, and ρ)
- scale for the shock affecting the reserve and civilian states individually (λ_1)
- scale for the dispersion of the shock affecting each different contract commitment length (λ_2) for the Navy. This parameter is zero for the Army because Army SOF officers were not offered continuation pay or retention bonuses that were contingent on a contract commitment

---

[3] This means that all relevant information from past outcomes is represented in the current state vector, which, in our case, includes years of AC service, years of reserve service, and taste.

- scale for the total shock, including the shock of the between-nest and within-nest choices

$$\kappa = \sqrt{\lambda_1^2 + \tau_1^2} = \sqrt{\lambda_2^2 + \tau_2^2},$$

where τ is the scale parameter of the nest-level shock (note that, for the Army model, there are no within-nest choices for obligation length), so

$$\kappa = \sqrt{\lambda_1^2 + \tau_1^2}$$

- a parameter, δ, that reflects the additional opportunities available to SOF members when strength levels increase (assumed zero for the Navy)
- switching cost incurred if the individual leaves the AC before completing ADSO
- switching cost incurred if the individual moves from "civilian" to "reserve."

Also, we typically estimate a personal discount factor, β, in the DRM. However, we found the model fits improved by fixing the personal discount factor. In past work, we estimated a discount factor of about 0.94 for Army and Navy officers (see Asch, Hosek, Mattock, 2013, Table C.4), so we set β to 0.94 in our SOF models.

Regarding the first switching cost, the completion of the first ADSO for Army SOF personnel typically occurs at YOS 8, given a four-year obligation and the fact that Army SOF officers typically join the SOF community at YOS 5 or 6 in our data. For the Navy, we assumed the completion of the first ADSO is at YOS 5, given that Navy SOF typically join the SOF community at YOS 1. The rationale for these assumptions is discussed in Chapter Four.

Once we had parameter estimates for a well-fitting model, we used the logic of the model and the estimated parameters to simulate the AC cumulative probability of retention to each YOS in the steady state for a given policy environment, such as the introduction of a new S&I pay or a change in the level of the pay. By *steady state*, we mean when all members have spent their entire careers are under the policy environment being considered. The simulation output includes a graph of the AC retention profile by YOS. We can also produce graphs of reserve component participation and provide computations of costs, although we do not do so here. We show model fit by simulating the steady-state retention profile in the current policy environment and comparing it with the retention profile observed in the data.[4]

---

[4] Our use of the term *steady state* differs from usage in dynamic models, where it refers to point(s) such that the vector of state variables, regardless of starting value, has converged to a value that is unchanging over time. The system is said to be in a steady state when the state vector regenerates itself period after period. In our use, the retention profile is in a steady state when it would be realized for successive entering cohorts. This occurs when every cohort has the same taste distribution, same shock distributions, and same personnel management and compensation policy. In other research (Asch, Mattock, and Hosek, 2013), we studied the effect of introducing a new policy and allowing incumbent personnel to opt in to the new policy or remain under the baseline policy. The overall retention profile evolves from the profile under the baseline policy to the profile under the new policy as more and more cohorts enter under the new policy and depending on how many incumbent personnel opt in. Finally, a maintained assumption in our analyses is that the taste and shock distributions and personnel management policy remain the same from cohort to cohort. As a result, the retention profile (the percentage retained to each YOS) would be the same from cohort to cohort so long as the compensation policy remained the same. Notably, the retention profile would not depend on the size of the cohort. We recognize that policy changes could change the taste distribution of entering cohorts and perhaps change the shock distribution. For instance, a large increase in the size of an entering cohort might result in recruits having, on average, a lower taste for military service due to recruiters having to dig deeper into the taste distribution of the eligible youth population than for smaller entering cohorts.

CHAPTER FOUR

Data and Military and Civilian Earnings Profiles

Data

We estimated SOF officer retention models using DMDC's WEX data, which contain person-specific longitudinal records of active and reserve service. We pulled records for any individual with a specialty code related to special operations (Table 4.1). The specialty codes in Table 4.1 were identified based on publicly available information on MOSs associated with the SOF community, including the DoD Occupational Conversion Index (Office of the Under Secretary of Defense for Personnel and Readiness, 2001).[1]

Our analysis file for each occupation includes individuals who were first designated as SOF officers (based on the occupational codes shown in Table 4.1) between 1990 and 2000. We followed the 1990–2000 officer cohorts through 2012, providing 23 years of data for the 1990 cohort and 13 years of data for the 2000 cohort. This initially identified 6,353 officers.

As discussed in Chapter Two and Appendix A, the Army and Navy exhibit fairly uniform requirements for accessions. Approximately 60 percent of the Army SOF officers in the 1990 through 2000 entry cohorts were first observed as SOF between 4.5 and 6.5 YOS (Figure 4.1). Similarly, approximately 65 percent of Navy SOF officers were first flagged as SOF (including SEAL trainees) during their first YOS, while another 20 percent were first flagged as non-trainee SOF in their second through fifth YOS (Figure 4.2).

In constructing our data for the Army, we started with the 1,814 individuals who were flagged as Army SOF officers and focused on the subset of officers who had been accessed into SOF during the typical part of an officer career.[2] Since officers can typically apply with three YOS, and training takes place during the fourth YOS, we limited the sample to officers who were first observed as Army SOF between YOS 4.5 and 6.5 (1,147 individuals). We also removed individuals who had prior reserve service (leaving a sample of 1,085), as well as those who remained on active duty as SOF officers for fewer than two years, which could indicate washing out of the program (leaving a sample of 856 officers). Finally, as discussed, the version of the DRM that we applied here does not allow transitions from the reserve or civilian states back to active duty, so we removed 69 individuals who rejoined active service after leaving.

This left a sample of 787 Army SOF officers from the 1990–2000 cohorts. Among these individuals, 403 were in the SF branch, and 340 were in the civil or psychological affairs

---

[1] We did identify 54 individuals in the WEX data who were flagged as SOF officers in the Marine Corps (with occupation code 0370). However, these individuals were only observed as SOF officers in 2011 and 2012 and were therefore not included in the cohorts we considered.

[2] We excluded individuals who switched between the Army and the other services during the period in which we observed them.

Table 4.1
MOS Used to Identify SOF Officers

Specialty	Occupation Code
Army	
SF	18A
PSYOPS, CA	37A, 38A, 39A, 39C, 39X
Navy	
SEAL Trainee (called "URL—Special Warfare, Trainee" in DoD list)	118X
SEAL (called "URL—Special Warfare" in DoD list)	113X
URL—Special operations (EOD/DIV/SAL/EOM)	114X
URL—Special operations, Trainee	119X
LDO—Special Warfare Technician	615X
CWO—Special Warfare Technician	715X
Special Operations/Low Intensity Conflict	2500 (SOC)
Commanding Officer, Special Warfare Team	9290 (DOC)
Executive Officer, Special Warfare Team	9291 (DOC)
Naval Security Group Special Operations Officer	9860 (DOC)
Naval Security Group Classic Owl Special Operations Officer	9865 (DOC)
Air Force	
Special Operations Pilots[a]	11SX
Special Operations Combat System Officers (called "Special Operations Navigator" in DoD list)[a]	12SX
Special Tactics Officers	13CX, 13DXB
Combat Rescue Officers	13DX
Special Operations RPA Pilot	18SX

NOTES: URL = unrestricted line officer; DIV = division; SAL = Strategic Arms Limitation; EOM = end of mission; CWO = chief warrant officer; SOC = secondary occupation code; DOC = duty occupation code.

[a] We also considered historical codes (valid prior to 1993) for Special Operations Pilots (1311, 1313, 1315, 1361, 1363, 1365, 1401, 1406, 1461, 1465, 1471, 1475, 1481, 1485, 1491, 1495), Special Operations Combat System Officers (1571, 1575, 1581, 1585, 2201, 2206, 2281, 2285, 2291, 2295), and Special Operations RPA (2511, 2516, 2521, 2524, 2531, 2534, 2541, 2546).

branches.[3] A small number of individuals (44) were observed moving between the SF branch and civil or psychological affairs branches.

For the Navy, we identified the 665 individuals who were flagged as Navy SOF officers.[4] Since most Navy officers appear to have been directly accessed into SOF positions (Figure 4.2), we limited the sample to officers first observed as Navy SOF in their first YOS (373

---

[3] We combined civil and psychological affairs because MOS 39A may include both branches.

[4] We exclude individuals who switched between the Navy and other services during the period in which we observed them.

Figure 4.1
Years of Service When First Observed as SOF, Army

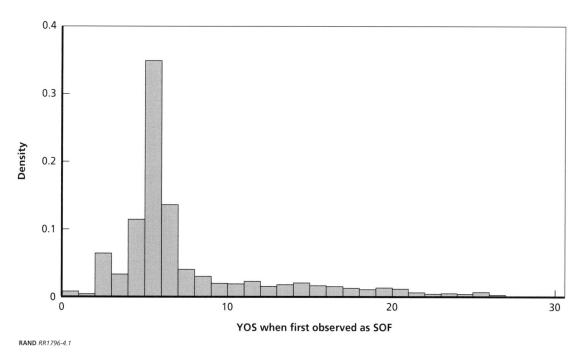

YOS when first observed as SOF

RAND RR1796-4.1

Figure 4.2
Years of Service When First Observed as SOF, Navy

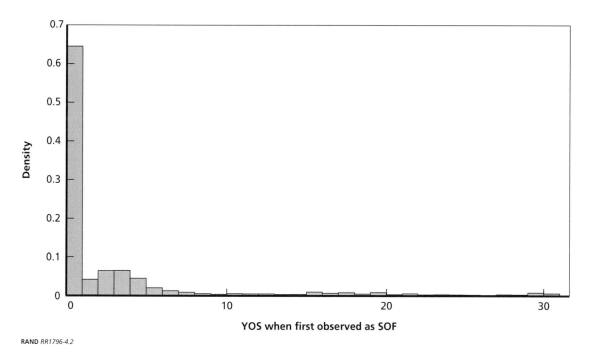

YOS when first observed as SOF

RAND RR1796-4.2

individuals). We also removed individuals who had prior reserve service (leaving a sample of 339), those who remained on active duty as nontrainee SOF officers for fewer than two years (leaving a sample of 297 officers), and those who rejoined active service after leaving (leaving a sample of 290 officers). We thus estimated the model with a sample of 290 Navy SOF officers from the 1990–2000 cohorts.

Military and Civilian Earnings Profiles

A key component of the DRM is a comparison of the pay at each YOS that an officer would expect to receive if staying on active-duty rather than leaving and taking a civilian position and potentially also a reserve position. Thus, we needed to develop profiles for military service and civilian work that showed expected earnings by YOS for an individual who stays in the military versus an individual who leaves.

A question we faced in developing the military pay line is what set of pays to include in the pay line we seek, "expected military pay." RMC is an easy choice to include. It equals basic pay, allowances for housing and subsistence, and the tax advantage of receiving allowances tax free. RMC is based on tables, which contributes to its predictability, and service members can expect its real value to be fairly stable over time because military pay must adjust in keeping with job opportunities in the economy to sustain the viability of the volunteer force. S&I pays may be less predictable, however. Some compensate for special skills, such as demolition, parachuting, and so forth, which are persistent features in SOF specialties and therefore predictable. The receipt of pays for hazardous duty is conditional on assignments or deployments involving hazardous duty, and these too are predictable, although probably more variable than skill-related pays. Also, the skill- and duty-related pays existed throughout the period covered by our data, with occasional but not frequent updating of their rates. In contrast, SWOCP and CSRB were introduced in 1999 and 2005, respectively, and CSRB was further updated in 2013. As mentioned, SWOCP and CSRB entail an obligation of military service and were used by the Navy but not by the Army.

Some insight into the role of S&I pay for SOF officers can be gained by considering average S&I pay, RMC, and gross cash compensation by YOS for SOF officers. Gross cash compensation includes basic pay, S&I pays, and allowances the member received. Allowances include the basic allowances for subsistence, quarters, housing and move-in, family separation, clothing, cost of living, and overseas. S&I pays include those relevant to the SOF community, as described in Chapter Two for the Army and Navy, such as Dive Pay; Parachute Pay; Assignment Incentive Pay; and, in the case of Navy personnel, SWOCP and CSRB.

We tabulated these averages using military pay and personnel data. Specifically, we identified SOF officers using the 2007–2012 Defense Enrollment Eligibility Reporting System (DEERS) Point In Time Extract files from DMDC. We linked these data to monthly active-duty pay files for 2007 through 2012 from DMDC and to annual Defense Finance and Accounting Service (DFAS) files for this period. The DFAS data include gross cash compensation for each member.

We identified 26,497 SOF officer-year observations in the September DEERS extracts, based on individuals having one of the service occupation codes given in Table 4.2 and a pay plan code indicating that the individual was an officer. Of the 26,497 observations, 22,182 appear in the active-duty pay files, indicating that the individual served on active duty for at least one month during the fiscal year (FY). We dropped a number of observations for the following reasons:

- 431 because they did not merge to DFAS data
- 1,097 for missing basic pay, allowances, or YOS
- 1,333 for missing gross pay
- five for invalid (negative) gross pay, basic pay, or allowance
- 648 for negative S&I pay[5]
- 318 for having fewer than 12 months of pay data in the active-duty pay files
- 4,558 for having fewer than 12 months identified as SOF officers in DEERS.

This left a population of 13,792 SOF active-duty officer-years.

Figure 4.3 shows the mean gross compensation profile for SOF officers in the Army, Navy, and Air Force by YOS. The Marine Corps is excluded because the sample size is small. All values are in 2015 dollars. The combined service pay line is the average for the Army, Navy, and Air Force combined. The Army pay line is close to the combined pay line, so using the combined pay line is much the same as using the Army line. But the Navy line is often above the combined pay line for 12 through 23 YOS.

Figure 4.4 suggests a reason for the patterns in Figure 4.3. It shows average S&I pay for SOF officers, by service and averaged across services, as a percentage of average gross cash compensation.[6] The percentages vary by service and illustrate their differences in the use of S&I pay. For the Army, average S&I pay is about 10 percent of cash compensation through 15 YOS

Figure 4.3
Gross Military Cash Compensation Profiles for SOF Officers in 2015 Dollars

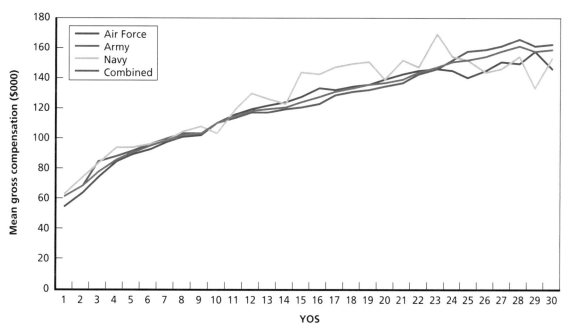

RAND *RR1796-4.3*

---

[5] There is overlap between exclusion categories. The numbers presented represent the number of observations excluded in the order in which they are presented. For instance, an individual who would be excluded for negative S&I pay and for missing gross pay would appear in the number excluded for missing gross pay.

[6] The DMDC pay files we received did not include elements for every S&I pay, so we derived total S&I pay as a residual from gross pay, basic pay, and the allowances: Total S&I pay = Gross Cash Compensation − Basic Pay − Allowances.

Figure 4.4
Mean S&I Pay as a Percentage of Mean Gross Cash Compensation for SOF Officers, by Service

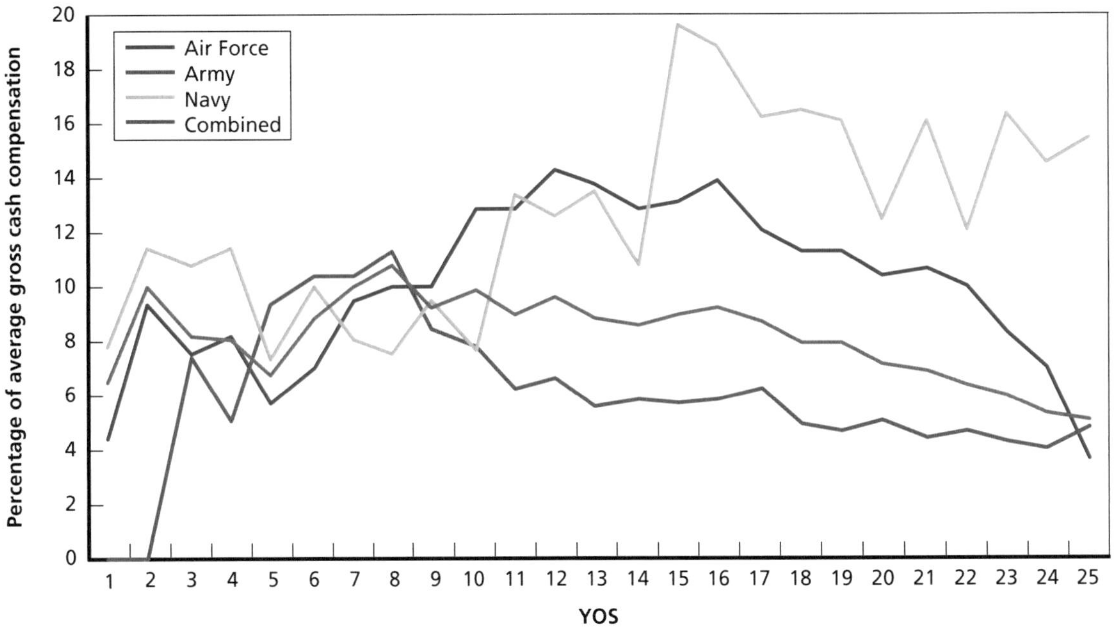

and then begins to decline. Army SOF officers receive S&I pay for diving duty, demolition duty, and other duties. Navy SOF officers also can qualify for these pays, depending on their billets, as well as for SWOCP and CSRB. SWOCP is offered from six through 14 YOS, and CSRB is offered at 15 YOS. For Navy SOF officers, the percentage of cash compensation from S&I pay is higher in 11 through 14 YOS than in five through ten YOS, and it goes even higher after 15 YOS, when personnel can qualify for the CSRB. (The percentage is relatively high in midcareer for Air Force SOF, between nine and 20 YOS, which could reflect the large number of personnel who become SOF officers in the Air Force during this phase of the career.)

Figures 4.5 and 4.6 show gross cash compensation, RMC, basic pay, allowances, and S&I pay for SOF officers for the Army and for the Navy, respectively. Figure 4.5 shows that S&I pay by YOS is small for the Army, on average, relative to average gross cash compensation for SOF officers, consistent with Figure 4.4. Mean total S&I pay typically ranges between $6,000 and $11,700 per year and tends to be highest between five and ten YOS. Figure 4.5 also shows that gross cash compensation for Army SOF officers is just above average RMC (which excludes S&I pay), indicating that S&I pay is a relatively minor element of gross cash compensation for Army SOF officers. Also consistent with Figure 4.4, Figure 4.6 shows that S&I pay for Navy SOF officers increases after nine YOS, especially after 15 YOS. Mean total S&I pay typically ranges between $8,000 and $27,600 per year.

For estimating and defining the military pay line for the Army, we used average gross cash compensation by YOS, as shown in Figure 4.5. For the Navy, we built the obligation choice associated with SWOCP and CSRB into Navy DRM and allowed the availability of SWOCP and CSRB to vary across calendar years, as described in Chapter Three. So, the expected military pay line for the Navy should exclude SWOCP and CSRB, since these elements of pay are already built into the DRM. That is, it is inappropriate to use gross cash compensation as the

Figure 4.5
Mean Gross, RMC, Basic, Allowance, and S&I Compensation Profiles for Army SOF Officers in 2015 Dollars

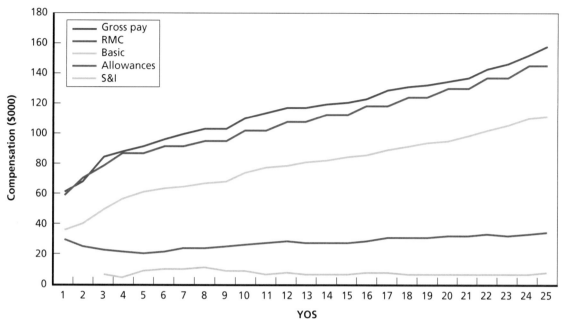

Figure 4.6
Mean Gross, RMC, Basic, Allowance, and S&I Compensation Profiles for Navy SOF Officers in 2015 Dollars

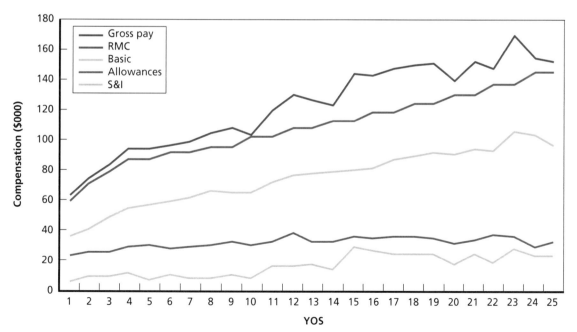

pay line for the Navy, as we did for the Army. (Note that, for the Army, it is unnecessary to build in the obligation choices associated with these S&I pays because the Army did not use SWOCP and CSRB.) Ideally, we would like to use a military pay line that includes RMC, as well as the S&I pays Navy SOF personnel receive that do not depend on a service obligation, such as those for hazardous duty and those that are skill related. Unfortunately, our data did not identify each of the S&I pays available to Navy SOF officers. We approximated the ideal pay line for Navy SOF officers with the RMC pay line shown in Figure 4.6 and used RMC as the pay line in the estimation of the Navy DRM.[7]

We also developed a pay line to represent the civilian earnings opportunities of SOF officers when they leave service. When SOF officers separate, they may seek a wide variety of civilian occupations. Some may choose security-related positions, and others may choose to capitalize on skills relating to foreign language proficiency, specialized knowledge of a specific region or country, or general management. Moreover, SOF officers making a stay-or-leave decision may not know what occupation they will want on leaving. Consistent with past implementations of the DRM (cited in Chapter Three), we used the 80th percentile of civilian earnings for men with a master's degree in management occupations in 2007 as an overall estimate of the expected civilian wage (DeNavas-Walt, Proctor, and Smith, 2008) put into 2015 dollars. We used the 80th percentile because past research showed that military pay is at about the 80th percentile of civilians with more than a bachelor's degree (Hosek, Asch, and Mattock, 2012). Put differently, military earnings exceed expected civilian earnings, consistent with the military needing to compensate personnel more than the alternative in recognition of the additional hardships of military service.

Figure 4.7 shows the civilian earnings profile used in our DRM analysis. It also shows the mean gross cash compensation SOF pay line averaged across the services and shown in Figure 4.3, although now relabeled as "military" for a simple contrast to the "civilian" pay line. Both profiles are in 2015 dollars. The civilian pay line is smoothed using regression methods.[8] Because we used the 80th percentile of those with more than a bachelor's degree, it is not surprising that military pay roughly equals civilian earnings, at least until YOS 20. Military personnel become eligible for retirement at YOS 20, and up-or-out rules become more selective. Consequently, average military pay after YOS 20 is conditioned on being promoted sufficiently quickly.

---

[7] As an alternative, we also estimated a Navy SOF officer DRM model using the Army gross cash compensation pay, under the assumption that the Army pay line included duty- and skill-related pay, as well as RMC, but not SWOCP and CSRB. We found that the model using RMC fit the Navy data much better, and we report the results in the next chapter.

[8] Civilian pay is converted from 2007 dollars to 2015 dollars by multiplying by 1.143, based on the Consumer Price Index Inflation Calculator (Bureau of Labor Statistics, undated).

Figure 4.7
Military and Civilian Wage Profiles for SOF Officers in Thousands of 2015 Dollars, All Services

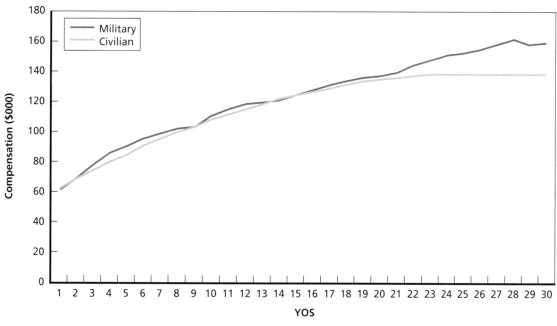

CHAPTER FIVE

Estimation Results and Model Fits

Table 5.1 shows the parameter estimates and standard errors for the Army and Navy SOF officer models. To make the numerical optimization easier, we did not estimate most of the parameters directly but instead estimated the logarithm of the absolute value of each parameter, except for the taste correlation, for which we estimated the inverse hyperbolic tangent of the parameter. All of the parameters are statistically significant in the Navy models, many highly significant, and all but τ and ρ are significant in the Army model. To recover the parameter estimates, we transformed the estimates. Table 5.2 shows the transformed parameter estimates for each service. The estimates are denominated in thousands of 2015 dollars, except for the assumed discount rate and the taste correlation.

We found that mean active taste is negative for the Army and equal to –\$61,220. A negative value is consistent with past studies estimating the mean active taste among military officers and suggests that the military must offer relatively high pay to compensate for the requirements of service on active duty relative to not being in the military. For the Navy, the point of estimate of mean active taste is negative but smaller in absolute value than for the Army, equal to –\$10,380. Both estimates of mean active taste are statistically different from zero.

The difference in estimated mean tastes for the Army and Navy is in part attributable to the difference in the military pay line used in the DRM for each service. As discussed in the previous chapter, we used gross cash compensation as the measure of military pay over a career for the Army, where gross cash compensation includes S&I pays. For the Navy, we used RMC, which excludes S&I pays. We explicitly modeled the SWOCP and CSRB choices in the DRM, so these pays are included in the pay line. But RMC excludes S&I pays that do not depend on a service obligation, such as Dive Pay. Consequently, the estimated mean taste for the Navy incorporates an adjustment for the role of these S&I pays.

Mean taste for reserve duty is negative: –\$35,660 for Army SOF and –\$39,470 for Navy SOF. As for the variance in tastes, we found that the standard deviation of active-duty taste is larger for the Navy than for the Army, \$12,030 for Army SOF and \$25,880 for Navy SOF, while the standard deviation of reserve taste is similar, \$18,900 for the Army and \$18,610 for the Navy.

The estimated scale parameters of the shocks in the Navy model are much larger than the mean and standard deviations of tastes. These scale parameters provide information on the standard deviation of the common random shock for the reserve/civilian nest, as well as the within civilian/reserve nest shocks. The model nests the reserve and civilian alternatives because most reservists also hold a civilian job; hence, a shock to civilian is also likely to be felt by reserve. The scale parameter for the active and reserve/civilian shock is given as $\sqrt{\lambda^2 + \tau^2}$,

Table 5.1
Parameter Estimates and Standard Errors: Army SOF Officers Starting SOF Career at YOS 5 or 6 and Navy SOF Officers

	Army		Navy	
	Estimate	Standard Error	Estimate	Standard Error
Log(Scale Parameter, Nest = τ)	−0.04	21.88	5.14	0.01
Log(Scale Parameter, Alternatives within Nest = λ_1)	4.48	0.08	4.97	0.01
Log(Scale Parameter, Alternatives within SWOCP and CSRB Nest = λ_2)	N/A	N/A	3.50	0.01
Log(−1*Mean Active Taste = μ_a)	4.11	0.11	2.34	0.30
Log(−1*Mean Reserve Taste = μ_r)	3.57	0.13	3.68	0.01
Log(SD Active Taste = σ_a)	2.49	0.29	3.25	0.31
Log(SD Reserve Taste = σ_r)	2.94	0.32	2.92	0.01
Atanh(Taste Correlation = ρ)	−0.06	0.22	−1.62	0.01
Log(Strength Parameter = δ)	−3.47	0.18	N/A	N/A
Log(−1*Switch Cost: Leave Active < ADSO)	4.55	0.08	6.33	0.18
Log(−1*Switch Cost: Switch from Civilian to Reserve)	6.21	0.08	6.63	0.01
Personal Discount Factor (Assumed)	0.94	N/A	0.94	N/A
−1*Log Likelihood	2,185		1,033	
N	789		290	

SOURCE: Parameter estimates from cohorts of SOF personnel entering active duty 1990–2000.

NOTES: The Army sample is restricted to individuals who entered SOF in either YOS 5 or YOS 6. The scale parameter governs the shocks to the value functions for staying and for the reserve-versus-civilian nest and equals $\sqrt{\lambda^2 + \tau^2}$. The means and standard deviations of tastes for active and reserve service relative to civilian opportunities are estimated, as are the costs associated with leaving active duty before completing ADSO, and switching from civilian status to participating in the reserves. For the Army, δ is the increment, denominated in dollars, in the value of staying associated with a larger strength. For the Navy, this switch parameter set to zero, since earlier analysis showed this parameter is not statistically significant. The personal discount factor was assumed to be 0.94 in these models.

while the within civilian/reserve nest shock is given by λ. Given that the shock is distributed Extreme Value Type I, the standard deviation equals the scale parameter times

$$\frac{\pi}{\sqrt{6}} \approx 1.283.$$

We estimate λ to be \$144,690 and τ to be \$170,650 for the Navy. These estimates imply that the scale parameter for the total shock, κ, is \$223,740. The relatively large magnitudes of the scale parameters suggest that movement into and out of active, reserve, and civilian statuses for the Navy is largely driven by random shocks rather than by diverse tastes among members (i.e., taste heterogeneity).

For the Army, we found that τ is small and not statistically significant from zero, so that the scale parameter for the active and reserve/civilian shock is essentially reduced to λ_I. We estimated a λ of \$88,190, roughly similar in magnitude to mean active taste of −\$61,220,

Table 5.2
Transformed Parameter Estimates: Army SOF Officers Starting SOF Career at YOS 5 or 6 and Navy SOF Officers

	Army	Navy
Scale Parameter, Nest = τ	0.96	170.65
Scale Parameter, Alternatives within Nest = λ_1	88.19	144.69
Scale Parameter, Alternatives within SWOCP and CSRB Nest = λ_2	N/A	32.99
Mean Active Taste = μ_a	−61.22	−10.38
Mean Reserve Taste = μ_r	−35.66	−39.47
SD Active Taste = σ_a	12.03	25.88
SD Reserve Taste = σ_r	18.90	18.61
Taste Correlation = ρ	−0.06	−0.92
Strength parameter = δ	0.03	N/A
Switch Cost: Leave Active <ADSO	−94.93	−559.72
Switch Cost: Switch from Civilian to Reserve	−496.31	−755.86
Personal Discount Factor (Assumed)	0.94	0.94

NOTE: Transformed parameters are denominated in thousands of 2015 dollars, with the exception of the taste correlation and personal discount factor. Definitions of variables are provided in Table 5.1 notes.

implying that tastes, as well as shocks, play a role in explaining shifts into and out of active, reserve, and civilian statuses for the Army.

The other within-nest scale parameter is for the SWOCP and CSRB nests for the Navy. This parameter, $32,990, is smaller than the other estimated scale parameters for the Navy. It is highly statistically significant and indicates that modeling SWOCP and CSRB contract length choices as nested choices was appropriate. The estimated scale parameter implies that the standard deviation of the shock to the SWOCP and CSRB nests is $42,309 (= 1.283 × $32,990).

The switching costs for leaving active duty early, before completing ADSO, are −$94,930 for Army SOF and −$559,720 for Navy SOF. The cost of switching to a reserve component after being a civilian is −$496,310 for Army SOF and −$755,860 for Navy SOF. The high cost of leaving active duty early may reflect the fact that individuals who accept SOF training are expected to "pay back" through service for the value received in training. The high cost of switching to a reserve component after being a civilian may reflect the difficulty of finding an available reserve position or an implicit cost to one's civilian career and lifestyle. Few individuals who have served as special operations officers in the Army or Navy make this switch in the data. Finally, the coefficient on Army SOF strength is $30, meaning that an increase of 100 SOF officers is equivalent to an increase in the nonpecuniary value of staying of $3,000.

Model Fit

To assess model fit, we used the parameter estimates to simulate the behavior of pseudo personnel represented by tastes drawn from the active/reserve taste distribution and subject to shocks drawn from a shock distribution with a scale parameter equal to the estimated value. Given active and reserve tastes, current-period shock values, knowledge of the expected pay lines in the military and the civilian world, and knowledge of the shock scale parameter, each pseudoindividual, behaving as a dynamic program decisionmaker, makes a stay-or-leave decision in each YOS in the AC. This generates a career length of service in the AC. After leaving active service, the individual becomes a civilian and makes a yearly decision regarding reserve participation. If the individual is not in the reserves, the decision is whether to participate; if the individual is in the reserves, the decision is whether to continue to participate. These decisions generate information about reserve participation by year for the years after AC service. We obtained the predicted AC retention profile by adding together these simulated AC retention profiles across a large number of simulated individuals, and we similarly combined individual reserve participation profiles to obtain the predicted reserve participation profile for the population of simulated individuals. The predicted profiles are plotted against the actual profiles to assess goodness of fit. Because both the Army and Navy models are cohort-specific, we can generate predicted profiles for each entry cohort, as well as a predicted profile that includes data for all the cohorts.

Figures 5.1 and 5.2 show the model fit graphs for active and reserve service for the Army and Navy, respectively; the Navy fit graph uses data for all the entry cohorts. The red lines are simulated cumulative retention, and the black lines are retention observed in the data. The figures show the Kaplan-Meier survival curves for the active components, and the dotted lines show the confidence interval for the Kaplan-Meier estimates for the observed data. In Chapter Six, we

Figure 5.1
Model Fit Results: Army SOF Officers in All Cohorts

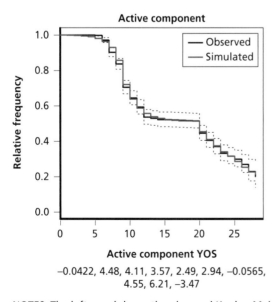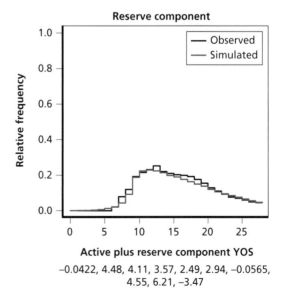

NOTES: The left panel shows the observed Kaplan-Meier survival curve and simulated active-duty survival curve. The panel on the right shows the observed histogram and simulated reserve participation histogram.
RAND RR1796-5.1

Figure 5.2
Model Fit Results: Navy SOF Officers in All Cohorts

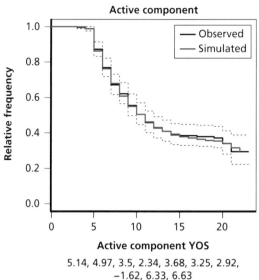
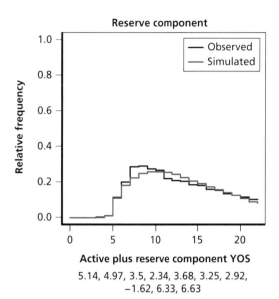

NOTES: The left panel shows the observed Kaplan-Meier survival curve and simulated active-duty survival curve. The panel on the right shows the observed histogram and simulated reserve participation histogram.
RAND RR1796-5.2

present simulated retention for changes in S&I pay through YOS 30, but our data did not extend to YOS 30, so the fit graphs do not extend to YOS 30.

In both the active and reserve graphs, the horizontal axis counts years since the individual was observed beginning active service. In the active graph, the vertical axis shows the cumulative probability of retention on active duty until that year. In the reserve graph, the vertical axis shows the cumulative probability of being in reserve service but not active service in that year, that is, the cumulative probability of being in the active or reserve service, minus the probability of being in the active service. The solid black line shows the actual retention of individuals in our cohorts, and the red line shows the predicted retention.

The model fit for the AC is quite good for both the Army and Navy, and the simulated retention profiles fall within the confidence interval or error bands of the observed retention curve. Army retention drops off after YOS 6 throughout midcareer and then stabilizes at YOS 12 until 20 YOS. Navy retention drops off more gradually after YOS 6 until YOS 14, when retention becomes more stable. The Navy offers SWOCP between YOS 6 and 14, so the more gradual drop-off for the Navy relative to the Army is not surprising. In both cases, the model predicts well the pattern of retention seen in the data.

The model fit for the reserve component is good for the Army and reasonable for the Navy. In part, this reflects the small sample size of Navy SOF personnel and the fact that relatively few affiliate with the reserves. The simulations in Chapter Six focus on the AC, where the fit is much better.

Chapter Six discusses how we developed simulation capability to model the retention response of SOF officers to S&I pay. We illustrate this capability for Army officers by simulating the retention response to introducing the CSRB to Army SOF officers, where the CSRB offered to officers is the same as the CSRB offered to enlisted personnel in career field 18. For Navy personnel, we illustrate the capability by showing the retention response to an increase in CSRB dollar amounts.

CHAPTER SIX

Simulations of the Retention Effects of Varying Special and Incentive Pay

Using the DRM estimation code and model estimates, we developed a simulation capability that allows assessments of the retention effects of changes in S&I pays for the Army and Navy SOF officer communities. We simulated the effects of a policy offering Army SOF commissioned officers the CSRB program currently offered to eligible Army SOF warrant officers and one of offering a 25-percent increase in Phase I and II CSRB bonus amounts for Navy SOF officers. These are not policies currently under consideration; we chose them to illustrate the simulation capability because they are ones that might be considered in the future.

We developed the simulation capability in the programming language R, then created a corresponding Excel-based capability that permits assessments of selected policy scenarios. The R- and Excel-based capabilities allow the user to vary the bonus amounts. So, policymakers can also explore the effects of a cut in bonus amounts for the Navy or, say, a 50-percent increase or a change in the bonus amounts under the SWOCP program for the Navy. Similarly, they can use the capability to explore offering different bonus amounts for Army officers than the amounts offered to enlisted SOF personnel. Moreover, the R-code and Excel capabilities can be adapted and updated to consider a range of other compensation policies, given the set of parameter estimates, including the effects of the blended retirement system or a change in military basic pay.

Army Officer Critical Skills Retention Bonus

We simulated the effects of offering the CSRB to Army officers, using the structure of benefits currently offered to Army warrant officers in Army MOS 180A (Special Forces).[1] For personnel with between 19 and 25 YOS, the Army offers: $18,000 per year for a two-year obligation; $30,000 per year for a three-year obligation; $50,000 per year for a four-year obligation; $75,000 per year for a five-year obligation; and $150,000 per year for a six-year obligation. CSRB payments are not allowed after 25 YOS.

Figure 6.1 shows the steady-state retention effects of the Army's warrant officer CSRB program on SOF officer retention. The results in the figure assume a strength level of 1,300 officers, equal to the median strength level between 2002 and 2012, as shown in Figure 3.3. The analysis assumes that there was no change in accessions to offset the change in retention and that Army SOF officers with between 19 and 25 YOS were eligible for the CSRB.

---

[1] See Department of the Army, Human Resources Command, 2015, for a description of this program.

Figure 6.1
Simulated Army Officer SOF Retention with CSRB Program

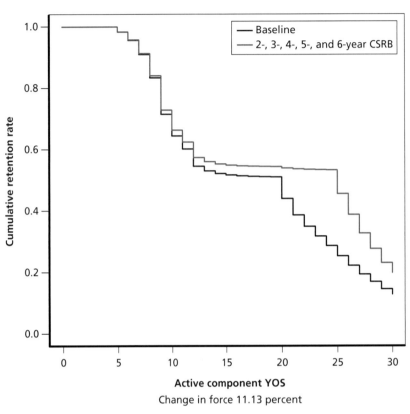

Change in force 11.13 percent

NOTES: Simulated survival curves for Army commissioned SOF officers assuming a
strength level of 1,300 officers. The baseline survival curve shows the estimated
curve based on the observed data, while the simulated curve estimates the change
in survival given CRSB for warrant officers, using the parameter estimates reported
in the previous chapter.
RAND RR1796-6.1

The analysis also assumes that the expected value of the CSRB is constant. Forward-looking
officers in early YOS anticipate that the CSRB will be available at its expected value as they
approach the YOS at which it is offered to them. A similar point holds for the increased Navy
CSRB that we simulate. We found that the policy would have a large effect on retention, with
an overall increase in Army officer SOF force size of 10.6 percent. Retention before 19 YOS,
when eligibility for CRSB first begins, increases a little as individuals in midcareer anticipate
the opportunity to take CSRB. The main effect of offering CSRB is to increase retention
after 20 YOS, effectively moving the large drop in retention from 20 YOS, when retirement
eligibility begins, to 25 YOS, when eligibility for CSRB ends. Thus, offering CRSB to officers
might substantially extend careers beyond 20 YOS. Important to note, this is the supply-side
response, indicating officers' willingness to stay. The increase in retention would not be realized unless the Army relaxed its retention control points so that SOFs could complete the additional service obligations they incur when they accept multiyear CSRBs.[2]

---

[2]   The Army does this for E-7 SOFs who take five-year CSRB at YOS 19 and might bump up against a mandatory separation point prior to completion of their obligations at YOS 24 (E-8 and E-9 high-year-of-tenure points would be nonbind-
ing). We thank John Warner for this point.

The 11th Quadrennial Review of Military Compensation examined the CSRB program for Army enlisted personnel. A study for this review found that the CSRB program had a large retention effect for Army enlisted personnel in infantry occupations (Warner, 2012). Specifically, Army enlisted SOF personnel remained in service an extra 4.5 years beyond 19 YOS on average with CSRB in effect. The Warner study used a difference-in-difference regression methodology and focused on enlisted personnel, but the results are qualitatively similar to ours. Both our study and the earlier study found that CSRB has a large effect on extending Army SOF careers beyond 19 YOS.

Increasing the Navy Officer Critical Skills Retention Bonus

To illustrate the simulation capability for Navy SOF officers, we considered a 25-percent across-the-board increase in the bonus amounts under the current Phase I and Phase II CSRB for SOF officers. For example, a three-year obligation in Phase I (between 15 and 18 YOS) would offer a bonus of $18,750 per year, rather than $15,000 per year, while a five-year obligation would offer $31,250 per year, rather than $25,000 per year.

Figure 6.2 shows the steady-state impact on Navy SOF officer retention, assuming no change in accessions. We found that a 25-percent increase in CSRB amounts would increase the Navy SOF officer force size by 3.71 percent, with most of the effect occurring between 15 and 26 YOS, when members are eligible to receive the CSRB. In the DRM framework, members are forward looking when they make retention decisions. Consequently, retention increases even before 15 YOS. Retention also rises a bit after 26 YOS because the greater number of personnel who choose to stay before 26 YOS increases the flow-through of individuals willing to stay after 26 YOS.

Figure 6.2
Simulated Navy Officer SOF Retention with 25-Percent Increase in CSRB Payments

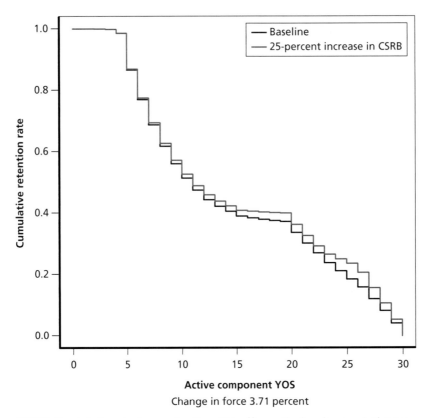

Change in force 3.71 percent

NOTES: Simulated survival curves for Navy SOF officers. The baseline survival curve shows the estimated curve based on the observed data, while the simulated curve estimates the change in survival given a 25-percent increase in CSRB amounts, using the parameter estimates reported in the previous chapter.
RAND RR1796-6.2

CHAPTER SEVEN

Wrap-Up

Our objective was to create a capability to predict how S&I pay for SOF commissioned officers would affect their retention. We adapted the DRM and estimated separate models for Army and Navy SOF officers. We developed a longitudinal database of active retention and reserve participation for each service for this community and reviewed S&I pay and developed estimates of expected military and civilian pay by age. We also reviewed the SOF officer career path in each service and adapted DRM code to handle service members' choice of the length of obligation under CSRB and SWOCP. The estimated DRM parameters were statistically significant, and the model fit the active and reserve retention data well overall. Finally, we demonstrated the capability of the estimated DRM to simulate the steady-state retention effect of counterfactual changes in S&I pay. The demonstration simulated the effects of changing the CSRB program, but the capability can consider other changes to S&I pay.

The completed research made progress toward meeting the project's objective but has limitations. The first concerns sample size and the number of years over which service members are followed. The sample included entry cohorts of officers from 1990 through 2000, followed through 2012. Service members were followed for as long as 23 years and as short as 13 years. In the future, it would be worth updating the file to follow personnel to the latest year available, currently 2016. This would produce longer files and additional cohorts of entrants, expanding the sample size for each specialty. The longer files might improve model fit in YOS past 20, although, as mentioned, the fit is already good. Second, the model does not control for changes in the pace of military operations. Deployments increased substantially in the past decade and have decreased since then, although the SOF community continues to be extensively used.

Third, the estimated DRM and simulation capability can show the effect of S&I pay on retention, but other data are needed to determine when the SOF officer supply is inadequate, or more than adequate, and trigger an S&I pay increase or decrease as appropriate. That is, the simulation capability is only one part of a system of information needed to adjust S&I pay. Fourth, changes in S&I pay type, availability, or amount could affect the size and taste of entering cohorts. The estimation assumed that the taste distribution was constant for the entering cohorts from 1990 to 2000. Future work could extend the model to allow for cohort-specific estimation of the taste parameters, sample size permitting. It could also address the effect of S&I pay, such as an accession bonus for SOF officers, to attract larger entry cohorts if desired. Similarly, the model could be extended to consider how changes in the pace of military operations affect the retention of these officers. Future research could also incorporate the cost of changes to S&I pay and assess the relative cost-effectiveness of these changes.

More Details About Special Operations Careers for Commissioned Officers

The special operations community of the U.S. armed forces consists of organizations within the four services that are tasked with conducting missions that require a greater degree of expertise, independence, or risk tolerance than would normally be acceptable for a conventional unit.

Although the selection, training, and career progression for officers in the SOF community are unique for each service branch (and between different occupational specialties, if a branch contains more than one type of SOF unit), there are some commonalities (Joint Publication [JP] 3-05, 2014). Additionally, there is some overlap in capabilities between services (e.g., ARSOF, Navy SEALs, and Marine Corps Critical Skills Operators are all capable of performing direct-action missions).

For the purposes of this research, we considered only officers whose occupational specialties are primarily considered to be USSOCOM assets and are expected to spend the majority of their careers in units that support USSOCOM. Thus, such units as Navy EOD teams and the Army's 75th Ranger Regiment (to name only two) will not be considered here either because their units do not directly support USSOCOM (in the case of EOD) or because their members do not spend the majority of their careers in SOF units (in the case of the Rangers, whose officers rotate between the 75th Ranger Regiment and conventional infantry units).

Additionally, we do not differentiate subgroups within the SOF community.

Army Special Operations Officers

ARSOF consists of three branches: SF, PSYOPS, and CA (USSOCOM, 2017). Additionally, ARSOF units are also supported by soldiers of other branches and MOSs who are not permanently part of ARSOF but rotate into ARSOF units (160th Special Operations Aviation Regiment and the 75th Ranger Regiment) on a temporary basis.

Special Forces Officers (MOS 18A)

SF officers (who are sometimes known as Green Berets) plan, coordinate, direct, and participate in SF units performing foreign internal defense, direct action, special reconnaissance, counterterrorism, counterproliferation, and information operations missions (see Department of Army Pamphlet 600-3, 2014, Ch. 16). Typically, these missions require SF officers to live and work closely with indigenous peoples and armed forces and require officers to be culturally astute, proficient in one or more foreign languages, and have specialized knowledge about a particular region of the world.

Psychological Operations Officers (MOS 37A)

PSYOPS officers are nonaccession officers who plan and execute information operations to influence the behavior of foreign target audiences (see Department of Army Pamphlet 600-3, 2014, Ch. 17). PSYOPS officers serve in both general-purpose and special operations forces but are considered to be part of the SOF community because they spend most of their careers in units that support USSOCOM.

Civil Affairs Officers (MOS 38A)

CA officers are nonaccession officers who plan and execute missions that directly engage and influence foreign civilian populations through civil-military operations, such as populace and resource control, foreign humanitarian assistance, civil information management, support to civil administration, and nation assistance (see Department of Army Pamphlet 600-3, 2014, Ch. 18). CA officers operate with other government agencies, foreign governments, and non-governmental organizations and are expected to be culturally adept and proficient in one or more foreign languages.

Other Army Branches Affiliated with ARSOF

Infantry officers who are qualified as Rangers and aviation officers may be assigned periodically to the 75th Ranger Regiment and the 160th Special Operations Aviation Regiment (SOAR), respectively.[1] The 75th Ranger Regiment is a light-infantry regiment that often supports the USSOCOM direct action mission (75th Ranger Regiment Public Affairs Office, undated).The 160th SOAR operates specially modified rotary-wing aircraft in support of USSOCOM missions (U.S. Army Special Operations Command Public Affairs Office, undated).Officers may be assigned to these units but are not themselves considered to be permanent members of the SOF community because they rotate back to conventional units.

Qualification Requirements

All three ARSOF branches are nonaccession and recruit applicants from within the Army during the first few years of the officer's career. Generally, one year group (YG) of officers is targeted at a time. Eligible candidates are reviewed by a centralized ARSOF screening board.[2] The following are the specific requirements for each branch:

---

[1]   Most infantry officers attend Ranger School during their initial accession training pipeline, prior to joining their first operational units.

[2]   The material in this subsection on qualification requirements is drawn from Department of the Army, Human Resources Command, 2015.

1. SF Officers[3]
   a. Be a member of the targeted YG. The Army typically releases an annual message targeting a year group three years prior to the current FY (e.g., the FY 2013 message will target YG 2010). This implies that the ARSOF Board considers only officers with three years in service.
   b. Possess a baccalaureate degree by the start of the qualification phase (if the applicant has passed the solicitation and assessment phases).
   c. Possess a Defense Language Aptitude Battery (DLAB) score of 85 or higher or a Defense Language Proficiency Test (DLPT) of 1/1 or higher in any language. The DLPT score must not be older than one year.
   d. Be Airborne (parachute) qualified or be willing to qualify before the beginning of the qualification phase.
   e. Pass the SF medical screening and be medically unrestricted. SF medical screening standards are more stringent than those for conventional forces (e.g., eyesight and color-blindness requirements).
   f. Possess or be eligible for a Top Secret clearance.
2. PSYOPS Officers
   a. Be a member of the targeted YG. The PSYOPS branch limits applications to officers with three years of commissioned service.
   b. Be selected for promotion to captain.
   c. Pass the Army Physical Fitness Test.
   d. Possess a DLAB score of 85 or higher or a DLPT of 1/1 or higher in any language. The DLPT score must not be older than one year.
   e. Be Airborne qualified.
   f. Be medically qualified per Army Regulation 40-501.
   g. Possess or be eligible for a Top Secret clearance.
3. CA Officers
   a. Be a member of the targeted YG. The CA branch limits applications to officers with three years of commissioned service.
   b. Possess a bachelor's degree or will possess a bachelor's degree prior to the start of CA training.
   c. Possess a DLAB score of 85 or higher or a DLPT of 1/1 or higher in any language. The DLPT score must not be older than one year.
   d. Be Airborne qualified or be willing to volunteer for airborne training.
   e. Possess or be eligible for a Top Secret clearance.

Although the minimal standards for the three branches are very similar, the Army officer community understands that SF applicants are held to a much higher physical fitness and performance standard than CA or PSYOPS officers. More generally, the screening boards (discussed later) that select candidates for training for each ARSOF branch evaluate these officers holistically, far beyond what the stated minimal standards are.

---

[3] Note that, while only male officers were being considered for accession to the SF branch as of this writing; the January 2013 removal of the military ban on women serving in combat means that the policy is no longer explicit. Male officers of any branch are eligible (i.e., the officer does not have to come from a combat arms branch, such as the infantry, to be eligible).

Accession and Training

These processes also vary depending on the branch.[4]

Special Forces Officers

Solicitation (195 Day Window)

The solicitation phase is roughly analogous to a written job application. The process begins when the Army Human Resources Command (AHRC) releases a message to the active-duty Army inviting candidates to submit application packages to the ARSOF Board. This message contains specific eligibility requirements, although these generally remain the same from year to year (as described earlier).

The military personnel (MILPERS) message that solicits applications is generally released in November. Applications are due the following February, and results are typically released in May. The solicitation phase lasts approximately 6.5 months (195 days).

Eligible applicants submit application packages to the ARSOF Board through the Special Operations Recruiting Battalion (SORB). The ARSOF Board will evaluate the applications and performance records. If the ARSOF Board recommends approval of a package, the applicant moves on to the next phase. Applicants who are denied are typically not allowed to apply again because their YG is considered only once.

Assessment (19 Days)

Once selected by the ARSOF Board, the SF applicant will attend Special Forces Assessment and Selection (SFAS), a 19-day-long screening course that is analogous to an extended job interview. The applicant will attend SFAS on temporary duty, away from his current assignment. SFAS is conducted ten times a year.

SFAS evaluates a candidate's intelligence, trainability, physical fitness, motivation, influence, and judgment through a variety of activities in high-stress environments. Because SFAS is conducted in an environment of limited information with no performance feedback, relatively little open-source information is available on specific SFAS activities.

Candidates who pass SFAS are assigned regional and language specialties and move on to the transition phase. Those who do not return to their original assignments.

Transition (Variable)

The transition phase has no comparable civilian analogue. This phase is intended to give the candidate time to complete non-SF career requirements. Generally, officers attend the Maneuver Captain's Career Course (MCCC), regardless of prior branch.[5] The course is conducted seven times a year and lasts 22 weeks.

After passing MCCC, a candidate who is not already Airborne qualified may attend Airborne training. The course is conducted 38 times a year and is three weeks long (U.S. Army Maneuver Center of Excellence, undated).

Candidates who have completed MCCC and Airborne training (if not already Airborne qualified) are ready to begin the qualification course.

---

[4]   The material in this subsection on the accession process and training is drawn from Department of the Army, Human Resources Command, 2015, and from Department of the Army, Human Resources Command, undated.

[5]   For example, an officer who was previously an engineer officer will attend the infantry-centric MCCC instead of attending the Engineer Captain's Career Course.

Qualification (357–399 Days)

The Special Forces Detachment Officer Qualification Course (SFDOQC) is a variable-length, MOS-producing (MOS 18A) school that prepares officers to lead an 18-man SF team. The school is divided into six phases: orientation and history, language and culture, individual training, MOS training, the culminating exercise, and graduation. Depending on the regional and language specialty of the officer (assigned in SFAS), qualification can take from slightly less to slightly more than one year.

Officers who complete SFDOQC are considered to be members of the SF Branch. Each immediately incurs a 36-month ADSO on graduation from SFDOQC and is then assigned to an SF Group. This ADSO supersedes any preexisting service obligation. For instance, an officer with a hypothetical 72 months of service remaining on an existing ADSO at the time of application who passes SFDOQC will have his service commitment cut down to 36 months starting from the SFDOQC graduation date. The same is true for existing ADSOs that are shorter than the 36-month commitment after passing SFDOQC.

General Notes on Pipeline Length

Under the most ideal circumstances (assuming that the applicant is able to attend the earliest scheduled course in each phases of the pipeline, is already Airborne-qualified, etc.), it takes one year and seven months for the individual to graduate from SFDOQC from the time the solicitation message is released.

Psychological Operations Officers
Solicitation (195 Day Window)

The solicitation phase is roughly analogous to a written job application. The process begins when AHRC releases a message to the active-duty Army inviting candidates to submit application packages to the ARSOF Board. This message contains specific eligibility requirements, although these generally remain the same from year to year (as described earlier).

The MILPERS message that solicits applications is generally released in November. Applications are due the following February, and results are typically released in May. The solicitation phase lasts approximately 6.5 months (195 days).

Eligible applicants submit application packages to the ARSOF Board through the SORB. The ARSOF Board will evaluate the applications and performance records. If the ARSOF Board recommends approval of a package, the applicant moves on to the next phase. Applicants who are denied are typically not allowed to apply again because their YG is considered only once.

Assessment (14 Days)

Once selected by the ARSOF Board, the PSYOPS officer applicant will attend Psychological Operations Assessment and Screening (POAS), which consists of situational training, a psychological evaluation, and physical fitness tests. Applicants who pass are afforded the opportunity to attend an appropriate Captain's Career Course before starting PSYOPS training. Candidates who do not pass POAS are returned to their original commands.

Transition (Variable)

After the candidate completes POAS, he moves on to the transition phase, which has no comparable civilian analogue. The transition phase is intended to give the candidate time to complete general career requirements. Generally, this consists of attending a captain's career courses—Maneuver, Military Intelligence, Military Police, or Aviation—depending on the original branch and ARSOF preferences.

After passing a captain's career course, the candidate may attend survival, evasion, resistance, and escape training if not already qualified in this area. The Army's intent is that captains (who make up the bulk of ARSOF officer accessions) be given the time to complete normal professional military education (PME) requirements that their peers (who are not in the middle of the ARSOF accession process) are fulfilling.

Qualification (287 Days)

The Psychological Operations Qualification Course (POQC) is an MOS-producing (MOS 37A) school that prepares officers to plan and execute psychological operations. The school is divided into four phases: introductory classes, language training, MOS-specific courses, and a culminating exercise.

Officers who complete POQC are considered members of the Psychological Operations Branch. Each immediately incurs a 36-month ADSO on graduation from POQC and is then assigned to command a PSYOPS detachment. This ADSO is concurrent with any preexisting service obligations, meaning that an officer will serve out the longest ADSO.

Civil Affairs Officers

Solicitation (195 Day Window)

The solicitation phase is roughly analogous to a written job application. The process begins when AHRC releases a message to the active-duty Army inviting candidates to submit application packages to the ARSOF Board. This message contains specific eligibility requirements, although these generally remain the same from year to year (as described earlier).

The MILPERS message that solicits applications is generally released in November. Applications are due the following February, and results are typically released in May. The solicitation phase lasts approximately 6.5 months (195 days).

Eligible applicants submit their application packages to the ARSOF Board through the SORB. The ARSOF Board will evaluate the applications and performance records. If the ARSOF Board approves the package, the applicant will begin the transition to the CA training pipeline without having to participate in an assessment exercise (as in the case of SF and PSYOPS candidates). Applicants who are denied are typically not allowed to apply again because their YG is considered only once.

Transition (Variable)

Once selected by the ARSOF Board, the candidate moves on to the transition phase, which has no comparable civilian analogue. The transition phase is intended to give the candidate time to complete career requirements. Generally, this consists of attendance of a captain's career course—Maneuver, Military Intelligence, or Military Police—depending on the original branch and ARSOF preferences.

After passing a captain's career course, the candidate may attend Airborne training if not already Airborne qualified.

Qualification (301–343 Days)

The Civil Affairs Qualification Course (CAQC) is an MOS-producing (MOS 38A) school that prepares officers to plan and execute CA missions. The school is divided into three phases: basic CA qualification, advanced regional analysis course, and language courses.

Officers completing CAQC are considered to be members of the CA Branch. Each immediately incurs a 36-month ADSO on graduation from CAQC and is then assigned to command a CA detachment. This ADSO is concurrent with any previous preexisting service obligations, meaning that an officer will serve out the longest ADSO.

Career Paths

Special Forces Officers

After SFODQC, the career path generally follows the same pattern as for non-SF peers. Promotion rates and timing for SF officers are similar to those for other branches, as outlined in the Defense Officer Personnel Management Act of 1980 (DOPMA; Public Law 96-513, 1980), and for other laws and policies governing military officer promotions generally. The permanent change of station (PCS) norms are also similar to those for the rest of the Army, with officers generally staying on station for 36 months before rotation, alternating between staff and command billets. PME and joint duty requirements are also similar to those for a non-SF officer.[6]

Psychological Operations Officers

After POQC, the career path generally follows the same pattern as for non-PSYOPS peers. Promotion rates and timing for psychological operations officers are similar to those for other branches, as outlined in DOPMA, and for other laws and policies governing military officer promotions generally. The PCS norms are also similar to those for the rest of the Army, with officers generally staying on station for 36 months before rotation, alternating between staff and command billets. PME and joint duty requirements are also similar to those for a non-PSYOPS officer.

Civil Affairs Officers

After CAQC, the career path generally follows the same pattern as for non-CA peers. Promotion rates and timing for psychological operations officers are similar to those for other branches, as outlined in DOPMA, and for other laws and policies governing military officer promotions generally. The PCS norms are also similar to those for the rest of the Army, with officers generally staying on station for 36 months before rotation, alternating between staff and command billets. PME and joint duty requirements are also similar to those for a non-CA officer (see Department of the Army Pamphlet 600-3, 2014, Fig. 17-1).

Navy Special Operations Officers

Overview

The Navy's primary contribution to USSOCOM is NSW officers (primary MOS [PMOS] 113X), better known as SEAL officers, falling under the Naval Special Warfare Command.

Naval Special Warfare Officers (PMOS 113X)

NSW officers plan, direct, and execute UW, direct action, counterterrorism, special reconnaissance, foreign internal defense, information warfare, security assistance, counterdrug operations, personnel recovery, and hydrographic reconnaissance missions (JP 3-05, 2014). These missions are similar to some missions assigned to Army SF and MARSOC units but are typi-

---

[6]   For a detailed guide to a typical SF officer's career path, see Department of the Army Pamphlet 600-3, 2014, Fig. 16-1.

cally conducted in amphibious or littoral environments. However, it is also not uncommon for NSW officers to conduct mission that would normally be considered the purview of Army SF or MARSOC (e.g., the Osama bin Laden raid).

Qualification Requirements

NSW officers are accessed either directly from their commissioning source (Officer Candidate School, Naval ROTC, U.S. Naval Academy) or, in limited numbers, from lateral transfers from within the Navy. Additionally, in rare cases, NSW officers have been accessed from interservice academy transfers (U.S. Military Academy, U.S. Air Force Academy) and interservice lateral transfers. (We will not discuss the latter group separately here.)[7]

Generally, before being considered for duty as a SEAL officer, applicants must

1. be between 19 and 28 years old (waived for prior enlisted SEALs)
2. possess a bachelor's degree
3. pass the NSW Special Operations Duty Medical Examination
4. be able to pass minimum physical fitness standards:
    a. 500 meter swim in 12:30 or less
    b. 50 push-ups in 2 minutes
    c. 50 curl-ups in 2 minutes
    d. 10 pull-ups in 2 minutes
    e. 1.5 mile run in 10:30 or less
5. agree to serve no less than three years of active duty as an NSW officer on completion of initial training (both BUDS/S and Basic Airborne Training); this obligation supersedes any previous service obligation.

Additionally, applicants who are already Navy officers must be

1. qualified in a warfare specialty (e.g., surface warfare, submarine)
2. O-1 or O-2 at time of application
3. on permanent active duty throughout the selection and transfer process.

All applicants must submit an application package that contains résumés, transcripts, and personnel statements to the SEAL Officer Selection Panel no later than March of the year they expect to begin training. A select number of applicants are interviewed by the panel through the summer, and final decisions are made in September. The panel selects individuals for training based on the "whole man" concept—considering academic achievement, physical fitness, foreign language proficiency, cultural knowledge, and recommendations. Once an officer has been selected for training, he is designated as an 118X.

Accession and Training

Officers whose applications are approved attend BUDS/S training (26 weeks) and Basic Airborne Training (three weeks).[8]

---

[7]   The material in this subsection on qualification requirements is drawn from Department of the Navy, Personnel Command, 2017, and Department of the Navy, Personnel Command, 2016.

[8]   The material in the subsections on accession and training and on career paths is drawn from Department of the Navy, Personnel Command, 2013.

After graduation, officers are assigned to either a SEAL Delivery Vehicle Team or a SEAL Team. Following a six-month in-house training and observation period, NSW officers will be examined, and their performance will be reviewed by their commanding officers. The designator for those found qualified will be changed from 118X to 113X. Those found unqualified either will be placed on probation for at least six months and then be reevaluated or will have their NSW designation and/or additional qualification designators revoked and be made available for reassignment.

NSW officers are encouraged to maintain their qualifications throughout their terms of service. Depending on their billets, they may be required to complete diving, parachuting, and demolition requalification at regular intervals. They may be eligible for Special Diving Pay and/or Hazardous Duty Pay.

In total, the accession and training process lasts about 203 days on average.

Career Paths

The career paths for NSW officers are similar to those for non-NSW peers. After an initial period of training, an NSW officer completes a tour as an assistant platoon commander of a SEAL platoon, typically reporting to his first operational command in his third year of service. He then alternates between further sea duty (with operational units) and shore duty (with supporting establishments). Promotion rates and timing are governed by DOPMA and other laws and policies governing military officer promotions generally. Joint duty and PME requirements are also similar to those of non-NSW officers.

Air Force Special Operations Officers

Overview

The Air Force contributes several types of officers to the special operations community: Special Operations Pilots, Special Operations Combat System Officers, Special Tactics Officers, Combat Rescue Officers, Special Operations RPA Pilots, and Special Operations Weather Officers. In addition, other officers, such as intelligence officers and pilots serving as Combat Aviation Advisors, may be selected to serve temporarily in AFSOC but are not discussed here.[9]

Special Operations Pilots (AFSC 11SX)

Special operations pilots fly fixed-wing and rotary-wing aircraft in support of special operations mission sets, such as UW, counterterrorism, direct action, and special reconnaissance. Unlike members of the Army's 160th SOAR, special operations pilots do not rotate in and out of units that are USSOCOM assets. The AFSC further breaks down into

- AFSC 11S4, Staff
- AFSC 11S3, Aircraft Commander
- AFSC 11S2, Qualified Pilot/Copilot
- AFSC 11S1, Entry/Student.

---

[9] The material in this overview is drawn from Air Force Instruction (AFI) 36-2101, 2017, and Department of the Air Force, 2017.

Special Operations Combat System Officers (AFSC 12SX)

Combat systems officers are flying officers trained to perform a combat systems, fire control, or electronic warfare officers in support of special operations mission sets (as defined earlier).[10] These officers are proficient in weapon system employment, defensive threat reactions, and electronic warfare. They also receive flight training but are not expected to serve in these billets. The AFSC further breaks down into

- AFSC 12S4, Staff
- AFSC 12S3, Qualified
- AFSC 12S1, Entry/Student.

Special Tactics Officers (AFSC 13CX)

STOs plan and execute ground missions, such as assault zone assessment and control, fire support, personnel recovery, combat search and rescue, battlefield trauma care, and tactical weather operations. They deploy as team members, team leaders, or mission commanders as direct combatants or to command and battle staffs to provide subject-matter expertise to plan and manage the command and control of special tactics forces. The AFSC further breaks down into

- AFSC 13C4, Staff
- AFSC 13C3, Qualified
- AFSC 13C1, Entry.

Combat Rescue Officers (AFSC 13DX)

Combat Rescue Officers are nonrated aircrew officers who lead and command personnel recovery operations as direct combatants. These officers act as mission planners and provide personnel recovery expertise to command and battle staffs on recovery operations, including survival, evasion, resistance, and escape programs. Combat Rescue Officers oversee the pararescue and survival, evasion, resistance, and escape enlisted career fields. Combat Rescue Officers manage day-to-day personnel recovery operations and organize, train, and equip assigned personnel to conduct rescue and recovery operations. The AFSC further breaks down into

- AFSC 13D4, Staff
- AFSC 13D3, Qualified
- AFSC 13D1, Entry.

Special Operations Remotely Piloted Aircraft Pilot (AFSC 18SX)

This AFSC is applied to officers trained to operate specialized mission aircraft and command flight crews to accomplish special operations, combat, training, and other missions. Regular RPA Pilots with the AFSC 11UX can receive specialized training in special operations and attain the suffix S, signifying that they are qualified in special operations. The AFSC further breaks down into

- AFSC 18S4, Staff
- AFSC 18S3, Qualified
- AFSC 18S1, Entry/Student.

---

[10] Before 2011, the term was *special operations navigators*, although the AFSC was the same.

Special Operations Weather Officers (AFSC 15WX)

Special Operations Weather Officers command, manage, and perform weather operations for Air Force and Army support organizations activities. They integrate current and forecast atmospheric and space weather conditions into operations and operational planning and develop, direct, and coordinate meteorological and space weather studies and research. They support and execute weather operations through leadership and management of weather groups, squadrons, flights, detachments, and operating locations and support the Air Force's core weather responsibility to provide meteorological and space weather information for DoD air, ground, and space operations. Weather Officers who receive additional training and specialize in special operations acquire the suffix "C." In addition to general 15WX training, Special Operations Weather Officers (who are designated 15W3C on graduation) require specialized knowledge of advanced field skills, environmental reconnaissance tactics, techniques and procedures, and leadership of small unit tactical operations in the joint special operations arena. The AFSC encompasses the following:

- AFSC 15W4C, Staff Special Operations Weather Officer
- AFSC 15W3C, Qualified Special Operations Weather Officer
- AFSC 15W1, Entry/Trainee Weather Officer.

Qualification Requirements

All prospective Air Force special operations officers may be directly accessed (OTS, Air Force ROTC, U.S. Air Force Academy) or laterally transferred from other communities (see AFI 36-2002, 2014).

Across the accession sources, candidates can volunteer for rated positions through a similar process. In Air Force ROTC, for example, candidates typically choose the rated position for which they want to volunteer during their junior year in college. They do so by providing a ranked list of the rated fields for which they would like to be considered. Selection decisions are made in the following order: (1) traditional pilot positions, (2) RPA pilot positions, (3) combat system operators (combat system officers, formerly navigators), and (4) air battle managers. For each career field, the top candidates are selected until all positions are filled. The remaining candidates are then considered for the next position for which they volunteered. The selection process creates incentives for candidates to volunteer for only the most desirable or high-paying rated career fields. Officers typically incur a six-year service obligation on graduation. Some officer communities have additional requirements:

1. Special Operations Pilots
   a. Pilots are evaluated on the basis of their Air Force Officer Qualifying Test, Pilot Candidate Selection Method score, performance on the test of basic aviation skills, and composite score based on previous civilian flight experience.
   b. Pilot candidates must also meet additional height, medical, and vision standards. The height requirements, which are based on the configuration of airplane cockpits, exclude many women.
   c. Candidates require an undergraduate degree with a specialization in a technical discipline (e.g., physical sciences or mathematics), with coursework in administration or management desirable.

    d. Females in this AFSC were, until recently, restricted from assignment to units below brigade level whose primary mission is to engage in direct combat on the ground (per DoD policy).

2. Special Operations Combat System Officers
    a. Candidates must be 29 years of age or younger.
    b. An undergraduate degree specializing in physical sciences, mathematics, administration, or management is desirable.
    c. Females in this AFSC were, until recently, restricted from assignment to units below brigade level whose primary mission is to engage in direct combat on the ground (per DoD policy).

3. Special Tactics Officers (see 24th Special Operations Wing, 2016)
    a. The STO community is only open to males (although following the January 2013 removal of the ban on women serving in combat, the policy is now unclear).
    b. STO candidates require a Secret clearance and must be eligible for a Top Secret clearance.
    c. Candidates must have an outstanding résumé and no negative personal history.
    d. Candidates must pass a Physical Ability Stamina Test:
        – 12 chin-ups or pull ups in 1 minute
        – 75 sit-ups in 2 minutes
        – 64 push-ups in 2 minutes
        – 3-mile run in 22:00 or faster
        – Swim 25 meters underwater
        – Swim 1,500 meters without stopping in 32 minutes
    e. Candidates must pass the IFC III Flight Physical examination.
    f. Candidates must be willing to incur a six-year active-duty service commitment (ADSC) on completion of the training pipeline.
    g. Candidates must be willing to volunteer for hazardous duty involving parachuting (static line and free fall) and combat diving duty.

4. Combat Rescue Officers
    a. Candidates must meet the general requirements for all Air Force officers. An undergraduate degree specializing in a technical discipline with courses in administration and management is desirable.

5. Special Operations Remotely Piloted Aircraft Pilot
    a. RPA pilots must meet the standards established for traditional pilots.

6. Special Operations Weather Officers
    a. Candidates must meet the general requirements for all Air Force officers.
    b. For award of AFSC 15W1, candidates require an undergraduate academic specialization in meteorology or atmospheric science or successful completion of the Basic Meteorology Program—a course open to U.S. Air Force Academy, Air Force ROTC, and OTS graduates who have met the minimum Basic Meteorology Program entry requirements of six semester hours of college calculus and six semester hours of college calculus–based physics. Alternatively, they must have competed 18 semester hours of college-level courses in meteorology, of which nine semester hours are a combination of dynamic meteorology and weather analysis and forecasting.
    c. For award of the AFSC 15W3A, officers must have completed a master's or doctoral program with an emphasis in meteorology and/or space weather science or have

completed 30 semester hours of graduate work with an emphasis on meteorology and space weather science.

Accession and Training

The material in this section is drawn from U.S. Air Force, undated.

Special Operations Pilots (882 days)

For entry into this community, Special Operations Pilots must complete either the Air Force Specialized Undergraduate Pilot Training or Joint Primary Pilot Training syllabus of training. The syllabus consists of general flight training and combat and water survival training, followed by specialized aircraft training, with an emphasis on training to accommodate the unique nature of SOF missions. On completing the pipeline, the officer is assigned to a special operations squadron.

Special Operations Combat System Officers (763 days)

Combat systems officers attend a series of schools similar to those for Special Operations Pilots. From the commissioning source, the officer completes water survival training, a modified general flight-training syllabus, and combat survival training, then specialized combat systems training for a particular aircraft with an emphasis on the unique requirements of SOF missions. On completion of the pipeline, the officer is assigned to a special operations squadron.

Special Tactics Officers (272 days)

STOs complete a six-phase training pipeline that begins with a ten-day selection course. An applicant who passes then proceeds to airfield operations training, followed by Army Airborne qualification, combat survival training, and tactical air control party training. On completion, the officer is qualified as a 13CX Special Tactics Officer and assigned to an STO squadron.

Combat Rescue Officers (319 days)

Combat Rescue Officers attend a ten-phase training pipeline that begins with a basic indoctrination course. If the applicant completes the course, he proceeds to combat dive school; Army Airborne training; military free-fall training; combat survival training; survival, evasion, resistance, and escape training; water survival training; underwater egress training; and finally a technical rescue course. Once an applicant passes all ten phases, he is qualified as a 13DX Combat Rescue Officer and is assigned to a squadron.

Special Operations Remotely Piloted Aircraft Pilot (292–382 days)

From commissioning, RPA pilots undergo a five-phase training pipeline that consists of basic piloting and instrument flying, proceeding to RPA employment fundamentals training, aircraft specialization training, and a joint firepower course. On completion of the pipeline, the applicant is qualified as an 18S3 and is assigned to an RPA squadron.

Special Operations Weather Officers (53 days)

Special Operations Weather Officers undergo the same training course as their non–special operations peers. From the commissioning source, the officer attends the 15W (Weather Officer) course and is assigned to a squadron for duty.

Career Paths

Air Force officers both inside and outside the special operations community have similar career paths and incur similar ADSCs. Special Operations Pilots (11S), like other pilots, incur a ten-year ADSC on completion of their rated training, which usually takes about two years following commissioning. RPA pilots (18S) incur a six-year ADSC on completion of their initial RPA training, which usually takes about one year.[11]

Combat Rescue Officers (13D), Special Tactics Officers (13C), and Weather Officers (15W) are regular officers, and their ADSCs are based on their commissioning source (five years for U.S. Air Force Academy graduates and four years for ROTC or OTS graduates). Personnel who complete the AFSOC Advanced Skills Training course or the equivalent incur a three-year ADSC, and those who withdraw or self-eliminate incur a two-year ADSC. These ADSCs are concurrent with all other ADSCs (Department of the Air Force, 2015).

Marine Corps Special Operations Forces Officers

Overview

The Marine Corps began contributing forces to USSOCOM in the mid-2000s and is in the process of building MARSOC. In particular, at the time of this writing, MARSOC is trying to define the career path for its Special Operations Officers.

Although a variety of officers serve in billets related to SOF-type missions (most notably Expeditionary Ground Reconnaissance Officers), only Special Operations Officers assigned to MARSOC units will be considered for this research.

Special Operations Officer (FMOS 0370)

Also known as Critical Skills Operator officers, Special Operations Officers (SOO) organize, train, plan, and employ MARSOC units from the team to battalion levels. These units conduct special reconnaissance, direct action, foreign internal defense, and counterterrorism missions. Additionally, secondary missions in support of information operations and UW are also commonly assigned to MARSOC (JP 3-05, 2014). SOOs are expected to be adept at working with partner-nation militaries.

As of this writing, SOOs did not have a career path. The Marine Corps solicits for SOOs across all officer PMOS populations. After qualifying and completing a tour of duty in MARSOC, these officers are then returned to their original PMOSs to continue their normal career paths. At this time, there are no plans to turn free MOS (FMOS) 0370 into a PMOS.

Qualification Requirements

The MARSOC accession pipeline for officers is a three-tiered process: solicitation, assessment and screening, and qualification. MARSOC does not recruit directly from the civilian population and is not a defined career path for officers. Rather, MARSOC recruits from the existing officer population and returns these officers to their PMOSs after their initial tour. MARSOC

---

[11] The material in this section is drawn from AFI 36-2107, 2009.

is in the process of determining how it will bring these already-qualified officers back for follow-on tours.[12]

Solicitation

The process for becoming a MARSOC critical skills operator begins near the third YOS. Officers wishing to apply for MARSOC must contact their base MARSOC recruiter and may do so at any time but generally do so during their third year of commissioned service. Currently, assignment monitors at Headquarters Marine Corps recommend that officers apply for MARSOC between their first and second deployments during their initial tour of duty (generally around the second YOS). The current eligibility requirements are as follows:

1. male officers only
2. either a career-designated O-2 or an O-3 with less than 1.5 years of time in grade (TIG).
3. minimum Army Services Vocational Aptitude Battery General Technical score of 105 (no waivers allowed)[13]
4. minimum Physical Fitness Test (PFT) Score of 225 out of 300 (regardless of age)[14]
5. no nonjudicial punishments during commissioned service
6. any derogatory administrative remarks regarding performance or conduct in the Service Record Book—"Page 11" entries—which require a waiver
7. no incidents of drug abuse or possession
8. no adverse fitness reports within 12 months of application
9. no court martial convictions
10. pass the NSW Special Operations Duty Medical Examination
11. must be willing to execute a 48-month obligated assignment on completion of Individual Training Course (ITC).
12. must possess a current Secret clearance.

Although not explicit, any male officer from any PMOS is eligible to apply.

Once an officer completes the application package, it is forwarded to MARSOC Recruiting. An Officer Selection Board convenes periodically to select officers to attend Assessment and Selection (A&S). This board generally meets 60 days prior to each A&S. Officers who are not selected may attempt to apply again, keeping in mind the upper grade limit of O-3 and the TIG limit of 1.5 years.

Accession

The accession process begins when an officer submits his application package (U.S. Marine Corps, 2015).

---

[12] This subsection is drawn from U.S. Marine Corps, 2007.

[13] The General Technical score is the sum of word knowledge and paragraph comprehension (verbal) and arithmetic reasoning.

[14] The PFT consists of three events: crunches, pull-ups (for males), and a timed 3-mile run. Each event is worth 100 points, for a total of 300 points. Each crunch is worth 1 point (100 crunches is the max score); each pull-up is worth 5 points (20 pull-ups max); and one point is deducted (from 100) every 10 seconds after 18:00 minutes on the run. According to MARSOC recruiters, successful officer applicants score around 290–300 on the PFT.

Assessment and Screening (45 Days)

If chosen by the Officer Selection Board, the officer applicant will prepare to attend A&S. This is considered temporary additional duty (also known as TDY) and is conducted three times a year at an undisclosed location. When an officer attends A&S is determined by consensus between the officer's current command (which will lose the officer temporarily during A&S) and MARSOC. Assignment monitors recommend that selection for A&S occur during the officer's second deployment (generally in the third year of commissioned service), so that the officer can attend A&S immediately after that deployment.

A&S candidates are tested on arrival in their ability to do the following:

1. score at least 225 on a PFT
2. conduct an abandon ship drill from a 6-meter platform
3. swim 300 meters continuously in utilities (excluding boots)
4. tread water unassisted for 10 minutes in utilities, followed by survival float using utilities for 5 minutes
5. execute a 12-mile forced march with a 45-pound load in four hours or less.

A&S evaluates its candidates in an ambiguous environment with no interaction from instructors, so information about the process is limited. Candidates who pass A&S are notified on completion and are issued PCS orders to attend the MARSOC ITC. Candidates who are unsuccessful may be invited back to A&S at a later date.

Qualification (246 Days)

Officers who pass A&S are ordered to Camp Lejeune to attend ITC, which has four phases:

- **Phase 1** (70 days) consists of basic skills training, including swimming; hand-to-hand combat; land navigation; patrolling; survival, evasion, resistance, and escape; mission planning; fire support training; combat casualty care; and communications.
- **Phase 2** (56 days) focuses on small-unit tactics, including small-boat and scout swimmer operations, crew-served weapon training. The phase and culminates in a two-week field exercise.
- **Phase 3** (35 days) focuses on close-quarters battle, with emphasis on rifle and pistol combat marksmanship and urban assault.
- **Phase 4** (49 days) consists of irregular warfare training, culminating in a field exercise that encompasses the entire training syllabus.

On completion of the course, officers remain at Camp Lejeune and attend Team Commanders Course (36 days), which focuses on the planning, training, and leadership skills needed to lead a 14-man Marine Special Operations Team. On completion of the school, officers are awarded the 0370 FMOS and are assigned to a Marine Special Operations Battalion to begin a 48-month tour of duty. At this time, there is a 60-percent combined pass rate for A&S, ITC, and the Team Commanders Course.[15]

Officers who do not complete ITC are eligible for reassignment by Headquarters Marine Corps.

---

[15] Personal communication with MARSOC, G-1, November 8, 2012.

No Dynamic Retention Model Estimates for the Air Force or Marine Corps

Air Force officers were first observed as SOF during various points throughout their careers (15 percent by two YOS, another 20 percent by six YOS, another 15 percent by ten YOS, and the remaining 50 percent after ten YOS); see Figure B.1. This suggests that a considerable portion of Air Force officers in the SOF community enter laterally after serving elsewhere, including the regular Air Force.

As shown in the figure, Air Force officers are first observed in SOF positions at widely varying points in their careers. Nearly one-half of the Air Force officers ever observed with SOF positions were first observed in these positions after ten YOS. The stay-leave decision for an Air Force officer with 12 YOS and two years of SOF duty is likely to be very different from that of an Air Force officer with five YOS and two years of SOF duty. Furthermore, estimating a DRM for retention over an Air Force SOF career would require incorporating the decisions of members outside the SOF community to stay outside, leave, or enter SOF laterally. That is, a DRM for Air Force SOF officers would need to be developed in the context of a larger DRM

Figure B.1
Years of Service When First Observed as SOF, Air Force

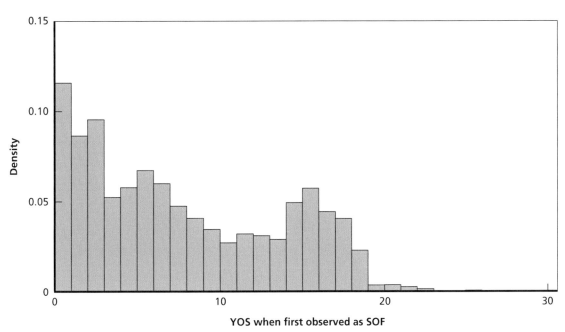

for all Air Force officers and would need to incorporate the decisions of Air Force officers to leave the Air Force or to stay and serve in the non-SOF Air Force or, alternatively, to serve in the SOF community. Such an extension of the DRM framework can be done conceptually and could be estimated with appropriate data but is beyond the scope our study. Therefore, we did not attempt an estimate for Air Force SOF officers but left this for future research.

We excluded the Marine Corps because we do not have retention data for a long enough time, given the relatively recent creation of MARSOC. Consequently, our DRM analysis focuses on the Army and Navy SOF officer communities.

Abbreviations

A&S	Assessment and Selection
AC	Active Component
ACP	Aviation Continuation Pay
ADSC	active-duty service commitment
ADSO	active-duty service obligation (Army)
AFSC	Air Force Specialty Code
AFSOC	Air Force Special Operations Command
AHRC	Army Human Resources Command
ARSOF	Army Special Forces
BUDS/S	Basic Underwater Demolition/SEAL
CA	Civil Affairs
CAQC	Civil Affairs Qualification Course
CSRB	Critical Skills Retention Bonus
CWO	chief warrant officer
DEERS	Defense Enrollment Eligibility Reporting System
DFAS	Defense Finance and Accounting Service
DLAB	Defense Language Aptitude Battery
DLPT	Defense Language Proficiency Test
DMDC	Defense Manpower Data Center
DOC	duty occupation code
DoD	U.S. Department of Defense
DOPMA	Defense Officer Personnel Management Act of 1980
DRM	Dynamic Retention Model

EOD	explosive ordinance disposal
FMOS	free MOS
FY	fiscal year
ITC	Individual Training Course
JP	Joint Publication
MARSOC	Marine Corps Special Operations Command
MCCC	Maneuver Captains Career Course
MILPERS	military personnel
MOS	military occupational specialty
NSW	Naval Special Warfare
OTS	Officer Training School
PCS	permanent change of station
PFT	Physical Fitness Test
PME	professional military education
PMOS	primary MOS
POAS	Psychological Operations Assessment and Screening
POQC	Psychological Operations Qualification Course
PSYOPS	psychological operations
RMC	regular military compensation
ROTC	Reserve Officers Training Course
RPA	remotely piloted aircraft
S&I	special and incentive
SEAL	Sea-Air-Land
SF	Special Forces
SFAS	Special Forces Assessment and Selection
SFDOQC	Special Forces Detachment Officer Qualification Course
SMU	special mission unit
SOAR	Special Operations Aviation Regiment
SOC	secondary occupation code
SOF	U.S. Special Operations Forces

SOO	Special Operations Officers
SORB	Special Operations Recruiting Battalion
STO	Special Tactics Officer
SWOCP	Special Warfare Officer Continuation Pay
TIG	time in grade
URL	unrestricted line officer
USSOCOM	U.S. Special Operations Command
UW	unconventional warfare
WEX	Work Experience File
YG	year group
YOS	years of service

References

24th Special Operations Wing, *Special Tactics Officer Application—Class 17-01*, 2016. As of May 17, 2017:
http://www.24sow.af.mil/Portals/80/STOappAugust2016.pdf?ver=2016-06-21-100742-243

75th Ranger Regiment Public Affairs Office, "75th Ranger Regiment," fact sheet, Fort Bragg, N.C., undated a. As of May 17, 2017:
http://www.soc.mil/USASOCHQ/Public%20Affairs/fact%20sheets/Fact%20Sheet%2075th%20Ranger%20Regt.pdf

AFI—*See* Air Force Instruction.

Air Force Instruction 36-2002, *Regular Air Force and Special Category Accessions*, June 2, 2014. As of May 14, 2017:
http://static.e-publishing.af.mil/production/1/af_a1/publication/afi36-2002/afi36-2002.pdf

Air Force Instruction 36-2101, *Classifying Military Personnel (Officer and Enlisted)*, March 9, 2017. As of May 14, 2017:
http://static.e-publishing.af.mil/production/1/af_a1/publication/afi36-2101/afi36-2101.pdf

Air Force Instruction 36-2107, *Active Duty Service Commitments*, February 17, 2009.

Army Regulation 40-501

Asch, Beth J., James Hosek, and Michael G. Mattock, *A Policy Analysis of Reserve Retirement Reform*, Santa Monica, Calif.: RAND Corporation, MG-378-OSD, 2013. As of June 21, 2017:
http://www.rand.org/pubs/monographs/MG378

Asch, Beth J., Michael G. Mattock, and James Hosek, *A New Tool for Assessing Workforce Management Policies Over Time: Extending the Dynamic Retention Model*, Santa Monica, Calif.: RAND Corporation, RR-113-OSD, 2013. As of July 7, 2017:
http://www.rand.org/pubs/research_reports/RR113.html

———, *The Blended Retirement System: Retention Effects and Continuation Cost Estimates for the Armed Services*, Santa Monica, Calif.: RAND Corporation, RR-1887-OSD/USCG, 2017. As of September 6, 2018:
https://www.rand.org/pubs/research_reports/RR1887.html

Bureau of Labor Statistics, "CPI Inflation Calculator," undated. As of June 22, 2017:
http://www.bls.gov/data/inflation_calculator.htm

Bureau of Naval Personnel, "Naval Special Warfare Incentives," via Special Warfare OCM webpage, 2014. As of March 2017:
http://www.public.navy.mil/bupers-npc/officer/communitymanagers/Unrestricted/nsw/Pages/default.aspx

Chief of Naval Operations Instruction 7220.16A, *Naval Special Warfare Officer Continuation Pay Program*, October 2015.

DeNavas-Walt, Carmen, Bernadette D. Proctor, and Jessica C. Smith, *Income, Poverty, and Health Insurance Coverage in the United States: 2007*, Washington, D.C.: U.S. Census Bureau, P60-235, August 2008.

Department of the Air Force, "Combat Rescue Officer AFSC 13DX: Career Field Education and Training Plan," February 1, 2015. As of June 21, 2017:
http://static.e-publishing.af.mil/production/1/af_a3_5/publication/cfetp13dxa/cfetp13dxa.pdf

———, "Air Force Special Operations Command (AFSOC) Core Missions," in Air Force Doctrine Annex 3-05, "Special Operations," Curtis E. LeMay Center for Doctrine Development and Education, February 9, 2017. As of May 14, 2017:
https://doctrine.af.mil/download.jsp?filename=3-05-D06-SOF-AFSOC-CORE-MSN.pdf

Department of the Army, Human Resources Command, "Officer Personnel Management Directorate (OPMD)," website, undated.

———, "FY16 Army Special Operations Forces (ARSOF) Officer Accession Panel Announcement (Regular Army)," MILPER Message 15-248, 2015a.

Department of the Army Pamphlet 600-3, "Commissioned Officer Professional Development and Career Management," Washington, D.C.: Headquarters, Department of the Army, December 3, 2014. As of May 16, 2017:
http://www.fa50.army.mil/pdfs/p600_3.pdf

Department of Defense 7000.14-R, *DoD Financial Management Regulation*, Vol. 7A: *Military Pay Policy–Active Duty and Reserve Pay*, April 2016.

Department of the Navy, Personnel Command, "Memon Key's NSW Career Path," slide, January 25, 2013. As of May 14, 2017:
http://www.public.navy.mil/bupers-npc/officer/communitymanagers/Unrestricted/nsw/Documents/SEAL_Officer_Career_path_template.ppt

———, "SEAL Officer Selection," website, May 2, 2016. As of May 14, 2017:
http://www.public.navy.mil/bupers-npc/officer/communitymanagers/Unrestricted/nsw/Pages/SEALOfficerSelection.aspx

———, "Special Warfare Officer Community Manager (OCM)," website, March 20, 2017. As of May 14, 2017:
http://www.public.navy.mil/bupers-npc/officer/communitymanagers/Unrestricted/nsw/Pages/default.aspx

DoD—*See* Department of Defense.

Hosek, James, Beth J. Asch, and Michael G. Mattock, *Should the Increase in Military Pay Be Slowed*, Santa Monica, Calif.: RAND Corporation, TR-1185-OSD, 2012. As of June 21, 2017:
http://www.rand.org/pubs/technical_reports/TR1185.html

Hosek, James, Shanthi Nataraj, Michael G. Mattock, and Beth J. Asch, *The Role of Special and Incentive Pays in Retaining Military Health Care Providers*, Santa Monica, Calif.: RAND Corporation, RR-1425-OSD, 2017. As of June 21, 2017:
http://www.rand.org/pubs/research_reports/RR1425.html

Joint Publication 3-05, *Special Operations*, Washington, D.C.: U.S. Department of Defense, July 16, 2014. As of May 17, 2017:
http://www.dtic.mil/doctrine/new_pubs/jp3_05.pdf

Mattock, Michael G., James Hosek, Beth J. Asch, and Rita Karam, *Retaining U.S. Air Force Pilots When the Civilian Demand for Pilots is Growing*, Santa Monica, Calif.: RAND Corporation, RR-1455-AF, 2016. As of June 21, 2017:
http://www.rand.org/pubs/research_reports/RR1455.html

Office of the Under Secretary of Defense for Personnel and Readiness, *Occupational Conversion Manual Index: Enlisted/Officer/Civilian*, Washington, D.C.: U.S. Department of Defense, DoD 1312.1-1, March 2001.

Public Law 96-513, Defense Officer Personnel Management Act, December 12, 1980. As of July 7, 2017:
http://uscode.house.gov/statutes/pl/96/513.pdf

Robinson, Linda, *The Future of U.S. Special Operations Forces*, Washington, D.C.: Council on Foreign Relations, Council Special Report No. 66, April 2013. As of August 29, 2016:
http://i.cfr.org/content/publications/attachments/Special_Operations_CSR66.pdf

Train, Kenneth, *Discrete Choice Methods with Simulation*, 2nd ed., Cambridge, Mass.: Cambridge University Press, 2009.

U.S. Air Force, "Flying Training Pipelines" website, undated. As of May 14, 2017:
https://www.my.af.mil/gcssaf/USAF/ep/contentView.do?contentType=EDITORIAL&contentId=c6925EC1A
C05F0FB5E044080020E329A9&channelPageId=s6925EC134A550FB5E044080020E329A9&programId=t6
925EC2C20EB0FB5E044080020E329A9
(Site requires a Common Access Card.)

U.S. Army Maneuver Center of Excellence, "Basic Airborne Course," website, November 12, 2014. As of May
14, 2017:
http://www.benning.army.mil/infantry/rtb/1-507th/airborne/

U.S. Army Special Operations Command Public Affairs Office, "160th Special Operations Aviation Regiment
(Airborne)," fact sheet, Fort Bragg, N.C., undated b. As of June 21, 2017:
http://www.soc.mil/USASOCHQ/Public%20Affairs/fact%20sheets/160th%20fact%20sheet.pdf

U.S. Marine Corps, "U.S. Marine Corps Forces, Special Operations Command (MARSOC), Recruit, Screen,
Assess and Select (RSAS) Process," MARADMIN 221/07, March 23, 2007. As of May 14, 2017:
http://www.marines.mil/News/Messages/Messages-Display/Article/890570/
us-marine-corps-forces-special-operations-command-marsoc-recruit-screen-assess/

———, "FY16 Headquarters Marine Corps MARSOC Screening Teams Schedule," MARADMIN 389/15,
August 7, 2015. As of May 14, 2017:
http://www.marines.mil/News/Messages/Messages-Display/Article/897353/
fy16-headquarters-marine-corps-marsoc-screening-teams-schedule/

U.S. Special Operations Command, *2017 Fact Book*, 2017. As of May 16, 2017:
http://www.socom.mil/FactBook/2017%20Fact%20Book.pdf

USSOCOM—*See* U.S. Special Operations Command.

Warner, John, "Evaluation of the Effect of CSRB Offered to Retirement-Eligible Special Forces Personnel," in
Report of the Eleventh Quadrennial Review of Military Compensation: Supporting Research Papers, June 2012. As
of June 21, 2017:
http://militarypay.defense.gov/Portals/3/Documents/Reports/11th_QRMC_Supporting_Research_Papers_
(932pp)_Linked.pdf